Get to the Top on Google

Get to the Top on Google

Tips and techniques
to get your site to the top
of the search engine rankings
– and stay there

David Viney

NICHOLAS BREALEY
PUBLISHING

LONDON · BOSTON

First published by
Nicholas Brealey Publishing in 2008
Reprinted (with corrections) 2008

3–5 Spafield Street
Clerkenwell, London
EC1R 4QB, UK
Tel: +44 (0)20 7239 0360
Fax: +44 (0)20 7239 0370

20 Park Plaza, Suite 1115A
Boston
MA 02116, USA
Tel: (888) BREALEY
Fax: (617) 523 3708

www.nicholasbrealey.com
www.seo-expert-services.co.uk

ISBN: 978-1-85788-502-6

British Library Cataloguing in Publication Data
A catalogue record for this book is available from the
British Library.

FSC

Printed in the UK by Clays Ltd on
Forest Stewardship Council certified paper.

Contents

Foreword

Search engine optimization (or SEO for short) is the art of getting your website to the top of the search rankings. Why would you want to get to the top on Google? Well, here is my elevator pitch for why SEO (and this book) could be the best investment you ever make in your website and your business:

⟡ Search engines are the way in which 90% of people locate the internet resources they need and Google has a 75% market share in Europe and North America. The Google brand is now rated as the most powerful in the world and, within three years, the company is expected to be the largest advertiser (by revenue) in the world. My approach focuses on Google because it's the most important, but includes tips on other search engines where relevant.

⟡ 84% of searchers never make it past the bottom of page two of Google and 65% of people never click on paid (or "sponsored") results. Being at the top of the nonpaid (or "organic") search results is a make-or-break mission for the modern business in a world ever more dominated by the internet.

⟡ Around 15% of all sales in the British economy are now completed online, and price comparison service uSwitch predicts that internet sales will make up 40% of all purchases by the year 2020. The numbers are similar in all the developed countries of the word, including the United States.

⟡ In this book I share with you my seven-step approach to search engine optimization and website promotion. This proven methodology is the very same process I use with all my clients (large or small, ranging from Amazon and Microsoft to the smallest high-street store) and contains all the tips and tricks you need to achieve top rankings. The rest is down to you: your effort, vigilance, and determination.

✧ Whether you have a new website or a long-established internet presence, there will be much in this book to challenge your thinking: not just how to promote your business but the very nature of your proposition online. The book is designed to be accessible for the beginner but comprehensive enough for the skilled marketer. You will be guided but not patronized.

✧ Throughout the book I use a case study to illustrate the seven steps. This helps you check your understanding and more readily apply the techniques to your own business. I also throw in six months of free membership to my SEO Expert Forum, so you can ask me questions and get direct help if you are struggling.

✧ I have set out to write the most complete and up-to-date guide to SEO on the market today. Unlike other, earlier books on the subject, this guide covers the emerging fields of Web 2.0 optimization, local search optimization, and the future of search itself (including emerging competitors to Google and alternative search models).

The SEO Expert website

One of the key issues with any book on search engine optimization is that the industry is changing rapidly and thus advice can become out of date before the ink is dry. The most successful techniques evolve over time and the tools available to the optimizer are improved, deleted, or replaced by others.

Consequently, I have made two commitments to readers of this book. The first is that new editions of the book will fully reflect and tackle developments in the search market generally and the Google algorithm in particular. The second commitment is that I will make available regular updates on search and SEO via my personal blog and business website.

The website at www.seo-expert-services.co.uk includes a number of features designed specifically to keep you updated, and gives you the opportunity to make contact with me directly:

- ♦ The SEO Expert Blog – a regular blogzine covering specific topics of interest or difficult challenges in the field of SEO. Any web user can view, syndicate, or subscribe to the feed (with updates via their newsreader, browser, or email).
- ♦ What I'm reading – a mash-up feed of interesting articles and blog posts from around the world direct from my own Google Reader account, mainly pages I have tagged on the blogs of other leading search engine marketers.
- ♦ The SEO Expert Forum – members can collaborate on their campaigns through a private forum and pose direct questions to the SEO Expert Services team, including me.
- ♦ The SES Toolset – members can access continually updated links to the best SEO tools, get discounts on SEO software, and download comprehensive lists of SEO-friendly directories, link exchange resources, and much more.

Membership of the SEO Expert Services site is free to all my clients. Nonclients can subscribe at the cost of £19.99 per month, for a minimum of six months. As a reader of *Get to the Top on Google* you qualify for a free six-month membership. To take advantage of this special offer, simply click on the "register" link on the homepage of the site, enter your details, and on the PayPal subscription page, enter the six-digit offer activation code 927406.

I hope you enjoy *Get to the Top on Google* and look forward to meeting you on my forum. Good luck with your website promotion and with the development of your business online.

Part I
Setting the scene

The size of the prize

84% of searchers never make it past the bottom of page two of search engine results. Just think about this for a moment. Imagine the web is one giant city, with stores scattered through it. Having your site in the top 10 is like having your store right on Main Street or near the entrance of the largest shopping mall in human history. Being outside the top 20 is like having a corner store on the very outskirts of town. Your footfall in a major mall is massive, with people coming in and out of your store all the time. On the web, a top position on Google has just the same effect.

Recent research has shown that the power of a top ranking is even more extreme than the 84% statistic suggests. Apparently, the nearer to the number one position your business gets, the greater the chances that you will actually convert your visitors to sales. It's almost as if web surfers associate a top position on Google with a quality brand.

A business very local to me (and dear to my heart) is the Teddington Cheese in southwest London. This unassuming little shop is rather off the beaten track for lovers of fine cheese. It isn't even on Main Street in Teddington. However, it does sell really excellent cheese from all over Europe and some aficionados come from miles around to take home a slice or two.

What many people shopping there don't know, however, is that the Teddington Cheese won a UK eCommerce Award and sells its cheeses to people all over the world. How did it achieve this? Well, one reason is that it is in the top 10 on Google for the search term "cheese."

I find the Teddington Cheese story inspiring. Although the web is less of a wild frontier than it used to be, there is still a place for a David seeking to take on the Goliaths of world commerce. You too can beat the big boys and afford that prime location right on Main Street, WWW. The keys are great product, sound service, niche focus, great content, and good search engine optimization or SEO – getting your site to the top of the search engine rankings. I can't help you much with the first four, but I can certainly help with the fifth.

There is a dark side to this heavy preference among consumers for a top-ranking company. More than once I have been contacted by businesses in desperation, who used to have a top 10 ranking but no longer do. I remember, in particular, a financial advisory business that used to rank top five for a wide range of loan search terms, and had grown from a one-man-band to a sizeable business in just a few years as a consequence. However, following a change in the Google algorithm (the way the rankings are calculated), its site had fallen out of the top 20, probably never to return, and it was ultimately forced to let all its staff go. The business was up against some very big banks with millions to spend, so regretfully I concluded there was little I could do (certainly within the much depleted budget available). Still, I will remember that desperation for a long time. Most problematically, the business had little substance to it beyond its web presence and had done nothing to build the capital or industry relationships necessary to sustain it through difficult times.

I tell this cautionary tale for a particular reason. I want you to remember that the web is only one channel for a sound business (albeit a hugely important and growing one) and that search algorithms are subject to constant change. Just because you're in the top 10 one week doesn't mean you'll always be there. Your competitors don't stand still. In fact, you have no god-given (or Google-given) right to a particular position. The search engines – and the traffic they bring – are fickle beasts. Forget this at your peril.

However, I do want you to be more excited than scared. I am passionate about the power of the internet and the potential it has to transform business, politics, and our entire society. As I have said, 40% of all sales could be online by 2020 and, with the help of this book, your store could be right on Main Street for millions of customers right across the world.

The seven-step approach

So search engine optimization essentially involves making it easy for search engines to find your website and boosting your position in their rankings. I use the seven-step approach to search engine optimization with all my clients and it has been tried and tested over several years with many different campaigns. It is an all-encompassing strategy, which allocates your time and energy appropriately across a range of valid and ethical SEO activities. Most importantly, it is correctly sequenced, so you do everything in the right order for maximum benefit.

There are essentially three phases to a campaign to improve your search engine ranking: planning and preparation (which includes keyword analysis and setting up your site), the campaign itself, and ongoing monitoring and maintenance. The process is iterative, so data gathered from ongoing monitoring feeds back into future campaign planning, for example. The three phases encompass my seven steps (see the table overleaf).

Each of the three phases needs to be given the appropriate focus. However, the first phase (Steps 1 and 2 in my model) is certainly the most important. In his book on military strategy *The Art of War*, Chinese general Sun Tzu said, "The opportunity of defeating the enemy is provided by the enemy himself." He also advised generals to "pick the right battlefield." So it is with SEO: You need to pick the right field on which to do battle and assess up front where your competition is most exposed. If you choose the wrong keyphrases to use on your website, for example, you are likely to expend a good deal of precious time, energy, and money on activities that will bring you scant return.

Before we go into the method in detail, I'd like to give you a brief overview of each of the steps so that you can orient yourself. You may find terms in the discussion that you don't understand, but all will become clear in the relevant chapter.

PHASE 1 PLANNING AND PREPARATION			PHASE 2 THE SEO CAMPAIGN				PHASE 3 ONGOING MAINTENANCE
Step 1 Phrases that pay	**Step 2** Courting the crawl	**Step 3** Priming your pages	**Step 4** Landing the links	**Step 5** Paying for position	**Step 6** Making the map	**Step 7** Tracking and tuning
1.1 Proposition development	2.1 How Google finds	3.1 How Google stores	4.1 How Google ranks	5.1 Match driver selection	6.1 Language optimization	7.1 Google Analytics
1.2 Keyword discovery	2.2 Setting up a new site	3.2 On-page optimization	4.2 Off-page optimization	5.2 Ad text optimization	6.2 Geographical optimization	7.2 Google Webmaster Tools
1.3 Keyword analysis	2.3 Managing an existing site	3.3 Asset optimization	4.3 What's new in Web 2.0	5.3 Landing page optimization	6.3 Google Earth and Maps	7.3 Other useful tools
1.4 Keyword deployment	2.4 Site structure and navigation	3.4 SERPs and snippets	4.4 Avoiding penalties	5.4 Campaign management	6.4 Priming for local search	7.4 Tuning the campaign

The seven-step approach

Step 1: Phrases that pay

Think of SEO as like cooking a meal. Keywords and keyphrases are your ingredients. Discovering <u>phrases that pay</u> is all about finding the right keyphrases for your business proposition, then deploying them for best effect in your site and campaign.

- ✧ <u>Proposition development</u> is about working out who your customers or audience are; what you can sell or promote to them online; how they will find your site; and what will convince them to do business with you.
- ✧ <u>Keyword discovery</u> is the first of three steps in my D–A–D keyword analysis technique. In discovery, you generate the longest list of possible search words and phrases your customers might use, with your competitors as a guide.
- ✧ <u>Keyword attractiveness</u> is the second D–A–D step and involves balancing keyword popularity and keyword competitiveness to determine the overall opportunity, or attractiveness, attached to each word or phrase.
- ✧ <u>Keyword deployment</u> is the third and final D–A–D step, where you use the principles of prominence, proximity, and density to work out how to chain, split, and splice together keywords into phrases that pay.

Step 2: Courting the crawl

<u>Courting the crawl</u> explains how to help Google to find your pages and index all of them appropriately, through building the right technical foundations and structure for your new or existing website.

- ✧ <u>How Google finds.</u> Your first important step in courting the crawl is learning how the Google spider, Googlebot, actually works and how to use sitemaps and robots.txt to initiate, control, and manage its crawl through your site.

✧ Setting up a new site contains vital information for new webmasters on how and where to host your site and how to select your domain name.

✧ Managing an existing site explains how to move your site to a new web host and/or move to a new domain without having an adverse impact on your website.

✧ Site structure and navigation concerns how to structure a site to the right depth and width to facilitate an effective crawl. It includes the optimization of your directory structure, file names, and file extensions.

Step 3: Priming your pages

Priming your pages covers the SEO art of page copywriting and asset optimization. This includes deploying your phrases that pay throughout your site and manipulating Google search engine results pages (SERPs).

✧ How Google stores. Before you can prime your pages you must understand how Google stores your content in its search index. This important chapter also covers the dreaded supplemental index and how to avoid it.

✧ On-page optimization is all about effective SEO copywriting of metadata, tags, page text, and other on-page elements, so that web pages are keyword rich for search engines but still read well for humans.

✧ Asset optimization. It is vital also to optimize the images, documents, videos, and other assets on your site. This section shows you how.

✧ SERPs and snippets outlines how Google displays its search results and how to manipulate the link and the snippet for your own pages, so that web surfers are enticed to click on the result and visit your site.

Step 4: Landing the links

Priming your pages is only a small part of the battle to get top rankings. By <u>landing the links</u> in a well-managed link-building campaign, you can go from also-ran to world champion and establish both the importance and the relevance of your site.

- ✧ <u>How Google ranks</u>. One of the most important sections in the book begins with an exploration of the Google algorithm (how sites are ranked or ordered within search results). It also covers PageRank, TrustRank, and text matching.
- ✧ <u>Off-page optimization</u>, the longest part of the book, incorporates strategies to build keyword-rich anchor-text links into your pages from other websites, so that the quality and quantity of your links exceed those of your competitors.
- ✧ <u>What's new in Web 2.0</u> explores how the emergence of hugely popular social networks has shifted the balance of traffic on the internet. The chapter specifically explains how you can use this to your advantage in your search campaign.
- ✧ <u>Avoiding penalties</u> is an introduction to the dark side of SEO: how to avoid using methods that could attract a Google penalty, and how to recover from and reverse a penalty if it happens to you.

Step 5: Paying for position

While 65% of people never click on paid (or sponsored) search results, 35% do. No comprehensive website promotion campaign is therefore complete without a full evaluation of paid search engine marketing.

✧ Selecting match drivers involves choosing the location, language, and time you want your ads to be searched in and selecting the phrases you wish to pay for (positive matches) and qualifying words you want to exclude (negative matches).

✧ Ad text optimization is the biggest challenge in copywriting: compelling a user to click on a link when all you have to work with are 25 characters for a title, 70 for the ad itself, and 35 for the URL. I show you how to achieve this most effectively.

✧ Landing page optimization. Your cost-per-click and conversion rates both benefit from well-written landing pages that deliver on the promise you made in the ad and channel the user through the rest of your site.

✧ Bid and campaign management is all about managing your campaigns, budget, day parting, bids, and ad variations to minimize the cost and maximize the return on investment. There's more to it than you might think!

Step 6: Making the map

As the web gets bigger, so searches become more locally focused. This innovative step shows you how to exploit this by improving your position for locally qualified searches and on local Google instances. It also covers Google Maps and Google Earth.

✧ Language optimization. If your site is multilingual, it is important that Google knows this. This chapter shows you how to tag pages and individual text blocks for different languages and how to get ranked in local-language searches.

✧ Geographical optimization. This may surprise you, but users narrow down 35–45% of their searches to sites based in their own country. This chapter covers the key steps required to rank well in these local search instances.

❖ <u>Google Earth and Google Maps</u>. In this chapter you learn how
to rank well in Google Maps and even Google Earth for local
searches – a vital piece of futureproofing for the increasingly
mobile web.

❖ <u>Priming for local search</u>. Many people add a place name to their
regular search query. This chapter shows you how to factor this
into your regular search campaign.

Step 7: Tracking and tuning

SEO is not a one-off process but an ongoing competitive struggle. You
need to monitor your performance objectively, using reliable data, and
feed this back into your campaign. This step shows you how.

❖ <u>Google Analytics</u>. Discover how to sign up for and use this
amazing set of free tools from Google: learn how to monitor
your paid and organic search traffic and track goal conversion
and campaign return on investment.

❖ <u>Google Webmaster Tools</u> is the all-in-one interface for managing
your crawl, monitoring your search rankings, and checking your
backlinks. Google continues to enhance this now invaluable
toolset.

❖ <u>Other useful tools</u> contains a round-up from across the web of
tools for tracking PageRank and Traffic Rank, plus how to interpret your own website statistics. The chapter also explains how
to use a Google API key, if you have one available.

❖ <u>Tuning the campaign</u> considers how to use the results of your
ongoing monitoring activity to refine your campaign further and
tune your site. It also looks at how to monitor what your competitors are up to and learn from them.

The rest of the book is essentially a walk-through of the seven-step approach, illustrated with a case study and punctuated with tools and resources. The longest sections, as you might expect, are those focused on on-page and off-page SEO, where I cover in some depth the key techniques you will need to master.

The Get to the Top on Google case study

Throughout the rest of this book I will be using a case study to illustrate the techniques involved and bring them to life. There is no single choice of industry or type of business that will readily surface all the challenges in search engine optimization. However, my chosen fictional example brings together the local vs. national optimization and both business-to-consumer (B2C) and business-to-business (B2B) aspects, so it manages to cover the bases quite well.

Meet Brad Chambers, brother of Matt Chambers, of Boise, Idaho. Older brother Matt took over the family printing business, Chambers Print, some five years ago, and it continues to deliver a healthy (although hardly spectacular) profit. The increased penetration of home PCs, decent laser printers, and the internet has made printing a more challenging market than in the good old days when their father, Ted, founded the company. Matt has to work harder and harder to maintain his top line and control his cost base. You can imagine, therefore, his mixed feelings at the news that Ted wants younger brother Brad to join the family business.

Brad, a recent marketing graduate from the University of Michigan, has a number of ideas about how to take the company forward. In particular, he wants to meet the challenges of the internet age head on by expanding the services offered via the Chambers Print website. As Brad puts it, "If you can't beat 'em, join 'em."

While Chambers Print sells standard stationery items, it makes most of its profits (90%) from bespoke printing; 55% of the profits come from small and medium-sized (SME) businesses and 15% from a single contract with one very large local law firm (Boise Law). The remaining 20% of profits come from the small or home office (SOHO) market, essentially a business-to-consumer space.

Almost all of Chambers Print's sales are made to customers within a 12-mile radius of Boise and most new business is gained by word-of-mouth recommendation. Matt has always focused on the B2B part of the business and, in particular, on winning larger contracts. However, it's now almost two years since the company won the Boise Law contract and there have been no new contracts of a similar size. More worryingly, the three-year contract comes up for renewal next year and Brad thinks it likely that Chambers Print will have to cut prices to retain the business (hurting its profitability).

In a nutshell, Brad thinks that Chambers Print could expand its operations over the internet to serve both businesses and consumers across the United States and Canada. He has an innovative idea to offer website users the ability to upload their own logos or artwork – something he has seen other sites doing with some success.

We will see how Brad develops the business – and calms his brother's misgivings – through the power of decent proposition development, search engine optimization, and more traditional marketing techniques.

So, now it's time to get cracking. The following seven steps (each containing four sections) walk you through the nuts and bolts of the art of search engine optimization – how to get to the top on Google and stay there!

Part II

The seven-step approach

Phase 1
Planning and preparation

Step 1: Phrases that pay

The first of two steps in the planning and preparation of your SEO campaign, <u>phrases that pay</u> is all about finding the right keyphrases for your business proposition, then deploying them for best effect in your site and campaign.

In this step we look at who your customers are and what you can offer them online. Using the D–A–D (discovery–attractiveness–deployment) model of keyword analysis, we then work out what search phrases they might use to find you – and your competitors.

1.1 Proposition development

Many companies start their online business presence by buying a domain name (a name for their website, often one close to their business name) and building a web page that is really little more than a brochure. Only later do they turn their mind to optimizing their site for both their audience and the way those in their audience find them. Very few take a long, hard look at what their online competitors are doing first or think about what part of their business works best online. And hardly any revisit their entire business model to consider how it might change to take advantage of what the internet offers. Take it from me, the best way to succeed in search engine optimization is to build it into your business development strategy from the very outset.

More importantly, an SEO campaign must be a means to an end, not an end in itself. It is vital to see it in its broader business context: What sort of visitors will convert well for this business online? Is the ideal visitor budget conscious or seeking luxury items? After all, there is no point in chasing high search volumes only to find that visitors look at one page, then leave the site. And don't let SEO take over your life – you still have to be out there doing business. It's easy to become hypnotized by the challenge and forget that SEO is only, at the end of the day, one part of your marketing effort; which is, in itself, only one part of the total business effort required.

For these reasons and more, before we turn to search phrases and optimization techniques, this guide considers those fundamental questions of what, who, and where.

What are you selling?

The first and most obvious question is whether you are selling a product or a service and the degree to which you can fulfill this online. Some service businesses are, by their very nature, intensely offline, local, and personal. For example, a hairdressing business will struggle to cut hair over the internet!

The best place to start is with what I call goal definition. A goal in this context defines a successful outcome from someone visiting your website and is expressed using a verb and a noun. Examples of possible goals include:

- ✧ Download a brochure
- ✧ Sign up for a newsletter
- ✧ Subscribe to a mailing list
- ✧ Request a product sample
- ✧ Book a sales consultation
- ✧ Purchase a product
- ✧ Book a service

Users can be grouped into the four areas of the marketing and sales funnel familiar to traditional marketers: a suspect, a prospect, a lead, and a sale.

Suspects are those who may have a (passive) need for your product and service. A suspect becomes a prospect once they have expressed an active interest in what you are offering. A lead is a prospect who meets the criteria of someone who is "ready to buy." A sale is "closed" when the lead becomes a customer and buys from you.

The goals in the list above really mark the progress of a user from one area of the funnel to another. Any searcher who finds and visits your site is a suspect. When they download a brochure they become a prospect. When they book a sales consultation they become a lead. When they purchase a product they become a sale.

As such, while a hairdressing business is unlikely to have "receive a haircut" as an online goal, "book a haircut" or "download example hair-styles" might well be part of its overall business proposition.

The most successful online businesses design a series of "customer journeys" through their site, which take a user from entrance to information to goal completion. Each journey begins with a landing page and ends with a so-called money page, where the user completes a goal. Each site may have several (often intersecting) journeys.

Later, in the section on analytics (page 224), I will return to customer journeys and introduce you to funnel analysis, which looks at where users drop out of the journey. Through tweaks and improvements, this "journey leakage" can be reduced over time and the conversion of entrance to goal improved. However, for now I will simply reiterate that you must have a clear idea of what your goals are while developing your proposition.

In our case study, Brad begins with a detailed review of the Chambers Print website. At the moment, there is nothing that users can actually buy online. In fact, the only goal a user can complete is to fill out a contact form in the "contact us" section of the site. The form requires the user to enter their email address, so at least it provides a list of prospects.

Furthermore, there are no separate landing pages for the different types of products and services Chambers Print offers. Instead, these are grouped together on a "what we offer" page.

Brad decides to construct a series of customer journeys around the key products and services his business currently offers. He also decides to add a new product line whereby users can upload their own artwork or logos to the site, using a series of print templates. In future, people will be able to order business cards, letterheads, compliment slips, invoices, and purchase-order stationery online.

There are actually a number of elements of Brad's proposition that we will revisit in subsequent parts of this guide. However, the key point for now is that simply putting up a brochure of all Chambers Print's products and services is unlikely to be the best strategy. Brad has some specific and focused aims. By thinking about them now (and refining them) he stands a much better chance of success online.

Who are your customers and what do they want?

Segmenting your audience is a key part of any marketing or PR strategy and, make no mistake, search engine optimization is essentially a marketing and PR activity (albeit somewhat different to some of the more traditional parts of this field).

Key questions at this stage (most of which will be directly relevant to your SEO campaign) include:

- ✧ Are your customers local, national, or international? How might this change in the future? Is language a barrier to them doing business with you?
- ✧ Are your customers business-to-business (B2B), business-to-consumer (B2C), or both? Do you need very different treatments for each segment? (The answer is probably yes.)
- ✧ Do your customers vary by demographic? Are they mainly of one sex or age bracket? Do they sit in any particular socio-economic class?
- ✧ Do your customers buy predominantly on price or on quality? Do you want to target upmarket users or appeal to the value end of the market? (Trying to do both at the same time rarely works.)

◇ Is time a factor for your customers? Do they need to buy
quickly? Do they only tend to buy at particular times of the
day/week/year or at particular points in their life?

◇ What is the potential for upselling customers into more expensive products? Or cross-selling them into different product
ranges?

◇ What is the prospect of repeat business? How many of your
customers are likely to form a long-term relationship with the
business?

Brad undertakes some fairly extensive market research, including
telephoning previous customers to find out what motivated them to
buy originally and why they did or did not return. He develops a
group of five different microsegments who will be the main focus of
the new website (and gives each a name, just for fun). These are
just two of the five, to give you a flavor:

◇ <u>Juan Manband</u>. Juan is a business of one, being both an IT
contractor and a home-based internet entrepreneur. He has his
fingers in lots of different pies and at least eight different business cards in his pocket that carry his name. He orders his business stationery and printing himself. He finds traditional printing
firms difficult to deal with as he doesn't need either logo-design
services or large print runs. He is cost conscious but also time
poor and tends to trade off the two. He is very willing to order
over the internet and do some of the work himself. He does not
need his printer to be local.

◇ <u>Cara Lotte</u>. Cara is personal assistant and office manager to the
managing director of a local business with 50 employees. She
handles everything from statutory accounts to payroll to
stationery and printing. She prefers the personal touch, local
suppliers, and people who keep their promises. She would use
the computer for research, but is suspicious of using it to buy

products. She looks for value (rather than the lowest price), putting a high emphasis on product quality. She would not expect to do any work herself.

In short, Brad has (like most businesses) identified both a local and a national angle to his online presence. He has also proved that there is indeed demand for printing over the internet on small print runs with rapid delivery. This will be his focus.

Who are your competitors and what can you learn from them?

No proposition development is complete without an honest assessment of what your competitors are up to. If you are in a locally based clicks-and-mortar business like Brad's, your assessment should take into account both your local and your global competition. Do a search on both your local Google and Google.com. Cross-reference this with data from Alexa (see the section on tracking and tuning, page 224). Focus on competitors that enjoy both good rankings and high traffic levels.

Ignore the SEO aspects for now and focus on the business ideas contained in your competitors' sites and how these are presented. A useful tool to use is so-called SWOT (strengths, weaknesses, opportunities, and threats) analysis, where you draw four boxes in a 2×2 table for each competitor. In the first box you note the strengths of the competitor, in the second their weaknesses, in the third their opportunities, and in the fourth their threats. Strengths and weaknesses are things inherent to their business as it operates today (and are generally internal). Opportunities and threats are things external to the business and are normally forward looking.

Look at each competitor website objectively and put yourself in the minds of your customers. Do you like the look of the website? Can you use it? Does it address each customer group separately, focus on one segment, or try to be all things at once? Is it easy to get information and do business? Before you become too obsessed with the SEO aspects, it is good to take some time out and get ideas from those who are already succeeding online.

Where and how will you win?

The internet becomes more competitive every day, but it is still a relatively immature medium that is evolving quickly. If you think it's hard to be on top at the moment, just wait until five years from now! Winning today is more and more about identifying a great niche and then ruthlessly pursuing a dominance in that niche. If you think about things from a business perspective first, your SEO effort will be all the more effective.

In summary (and to use a fishing analogy), look at what the more experienced anglers are doing. Copy what works but don't follow the crowd: Find a good stream that isn't overfished; stand where the current runs strongest; and use the right bait. Most importantly, keep the right fish and throw back the tiddlers for someone else to catch.

1.2 Keyword discovery

When a user visits a search engine, they type words into the search box to find what they are looking for. The search terms they type are called keywords and the combinations of keywords are keyphrases.

If you imagine that building an optimized site is like cooking a meal, then keywords are the essential ingredients. Would you attempt to cook a complex new dish without first referring to a recipe? Would you start before you had all the ingredients available and properly prepared? In our analogy, keywords are your ingredients and the rest of the seven-step approach is your recipe.

Ideally, you should undertake keyword research well before you choose a domain name, structure your site, and build your content. However, this is not always possible, as most webmasters only turn to SEO after they've built their site.

Even if you have a site already, it is vital to invest significant time and energy on keyword research before starting your SEO campaign. Although this may astonish you, I would recommend that 20% of all your SEO effort is focused on this activity alone. If you make poor keyword selections, you are likely to waste energy elsewhere in your SEO campaign, pursuing avenues unlikely to yield traffic in sufficient quantity, quality, or both. To return to our analogy, if you select poor ingredients, no matter how good the recipe may be the meal itself will be a disappointment – and no one will want to eat it.

Don't forget that one source for information about keywords is your own web logs. This helps you avoid undoing what you're already ranking well for. Google Analytics' keyword stats can also be particularly useful input to the early stages of an SEO campaign (see page 225 for more on this). I learnt this lesson from a client who ran a local catering business. She told me that many of her customers had found her via Google, but she couldn't understand what they were searching on as she could never find her site in the top 50, let alone the top 10. By investigating her Google Analytics stats, we discovered that she was ranking well for "thanksgiving catering" due to some client testimonials and pictures on her site. This explained why so many of her clients were ex-pat Americans and how they were finding her business; after all, such a search term was pretty niche in South West London, UK!

Common mistakes in keyword selection

Most people approach SEO with a preconception – or prejudice – about what their best keywords are. They are normally either wholly or partly wrong. This is good for you because you are armed with this book.

There are five key mistakes to avoid when selecting keywords:

1   Many of my customers first approach me with the sole objective of ranking number one on Google for the name of their business. Please don't misunderstand me, I am not saying that this

isn't important. If someone you met at a party or in the street could remember your business name and wanted to use Google to find your site, you should certainly ensure that you appear in the top five. However, your business name is very easy to optimize for and only likely ever to yield traffic from people you have already met or who have heard of your business through a word-of-mouth referral. The real power of a search engine is its ability to deliver quality leads from people who have *never* heard of your business before. As such, ranking number one for your business name, while it's an important foundation, is really only of secondary importance in the race to achieve good rankings on the web.

2   Many site owners (particularly in the business-to-business sector) make the mistake of wanting to rank well for very esoteric and supply-side terminology. For example, one client of mine was very happy to be in the top 10 on Google for "specimen trees and shrubs," because that was the supply-side terminology for his main business (importing wholesale trees and shrubs). However, fewer than 10 people a month worldwide search using that phrase. My client would have been much better off optimizing for "wholesale plants," which attracts a much more significant volume of searches. In short, his excellent search engine position was useless to him, as it never resulted in any traffic.

3   Many webmasters only want to rank well for single words (rather than chains of words). You may be surprised to hear that (based on research by OneStat.com) 33% of all searches on search engines are for two-word combinations, 26% for three words, and 21% for four or more words. Just 20% of people search on single words. Why does that surprise you, though? Isn't that what you do when you're searching? Even if you start with one word, the results you get are generally not specific enough (so you try adding further words to refine your search). It is therefore vital that keyword analysis is firmly based on

objective facts about what people actually search on rather than your own subjective guess about what they use.

4 People tend to copy their competitors when choosing the words to use, without researching in detail what people actually search for and how many competing sites already carry these terms. Good SEO is all about finding phrases that pay that are relatively popular with searchers but relatively underused by your competitors.

5 Many webmasters overuse certain keywords on their site (so-called keyword stuffing) and underuse related keywords. Human readers find such pages irritating and Google's spam filters look for these unnatural patterns and penalize them! Instead, it is much better to make liberal use of synonyms and other words related to your main terms. This process (often involving a thesaurus) is what information professionals call ontological analysis.

The best way to avoid these and other common mistakes is to follow the following maxims:

❖ Think like your customer and use their language, not yours.
❖ Put aside your preconceptions of what you wanted to rank for.
❖ Put aside subjectivity and focus on the facts.
❖ Consider popularity, competitiveness, and ontology.

In short, you need to make a scientific study of the keywords and keyphrases your customers and competitors actually use, and balance this against what your competitors are doing. I use a three-step approach to keyword analysis (known affectionately as D–A–D): discovery, attractiveness, and deployment.

Keyword discovery, the first step, is the process of finding all the keywords and keyphrases that are most relevant to your website and business proposition.

The D–A–D analysis tool

Throughout the steps of the D-A-D model, I will refer to a spreadsheet-based tool that always accompanies my keyword analysis. Create a new spreadsheet or table to record your work, with six columns (from left to right):

A Keywords
B Monthly searches
C Raw competition
D Directly competing
E KEI
F KOI

All will become clear later in this chapter.

In the keyword discovery phase, we are focusing on Column A only and trying to compile as large a list of keywords as possible.

The discovery shortcut: Learning from competitors

The place to begin your discovery is again by looking at your competitors' sites. Try putting into Google search terms related to your business, its products and services. For each of the top five results on each search term, select the "View source" or "View page source" option from your browser menu. Make a note of the keywords placed in the <TITLE>, <META NAME="Description">, and <META NAME="Keywords"> tags.

FORUM
TOOLS

Alternatively, if looking through HTML code (hypertext markup language, the programming language used to create web pages) leaves you cold, visit one of the keyword analysis tools listed on the forum that accompanies this book (www.seo-expert-services.co.uk). One good example is the Abakus Topword Keyword Check Tool: www.abakus-internet-marketing.de/tools/topword.html.

Here you can enter the URLs of your competitors and read off the keywords that they use.

List all of the keywords and keyphrases you find on your competitors' sites, one after another, in Column A of your spreadsheet. Don't read me wrong here. This kind of <u>metadata</u> (data about data, in this case a categorization of common terms), particularly in isolation, is not the route to high search engine rankings (as you will see later). However, sites in the top five on Google have generally undertaken SEO campaigns and have already developed a good idea of what the more popular keywords are for their (and your) niche. As such, their metadata is likely to reflect quality keyword analysis, repeated throughout the site in other ways. This effectively represents a shortcut that gets your campaign off to a flying start.

Search engines provide the modern information scientist with a hugely rich data set of search terms commonly used by people to retrieve the web pages they are looking for. I have coined some terms to help describe these that I use in my business.

<u>CUSPs</u> – commonly used search phrases – are phrases that people tend to use when searching for something and, more importantly, narrowing down the search results returned. There are normally two parts to a CUSP, a "stem phrase" and a "qualifying phrase."

For example, a stem for Brad might be "business cards" and a qualifier "full color." Additional qualifiers might be "cheap," "luxury," "do it yourself," and a whole host of other terms.

Sometimes qualifiers are strung together, in terms such as "cheap Caribbean cruises." And often people will use different synonyms or otherwise semantically similar words to describe the same qualifying phrase.

For example, "discounted" and "inexpensive" are synonyms of "cheap." However, searchers have learnt that phrases like "last minute" and "special offer" might return similar results. As such, searchers are just as likely to search for "last minute cruises" or "special offer cruises" as "cheap cruises." I use the acronym SEP (semantically equivalent phrase) to describe both simple synonyms and more intuitive variants, and Google is capable of recognizing both.

When undertaking keyword research, I tend to group CUSPs into SEPs and then group SEPs under the stem to which they relate. For example:

✧ Stem: Business Cards
  • SEP: Cheap Business Cards
           CUSPs: Inexpensive Business Cards, Discounted
           Business Cards, Special Offer Business Cards
  • SEP: Luxury Business Cards
           CUSPs: Premium Business Cards, Quality Business
           Cards, Handmade Business Cards

For speed, I often simply list the search phrases under a stem one after another, separated by commas.

> Brad searches for "business card printers" – and a small number of other keyphrases – on Google and takes a long look at the top 10 results for each search. He uses the menu option "View source" in Internet Explorer to look at the keywords used in the page metadata.
>
> He is surprised to find some consistent themes. For example, almost all of the top-ranked sites offer a way for users to upload their artwork or even to design it online. It seems he has not been the only person with this idea! He also finds a huge variety of keywords used and comes up with the following list (grouped under stems) to summarize his discovery efforts:
>
> ✧ <u>Business cards</u>: business cards, cheap business cards, free business cards, affordable business cards, discount business cards, business card design, full color business cards, folded cards, business card, business card printing, CD business cards, CD Rom business cards, caricature business cards, premium business

cards, luxury business cards, caricature contact cards, business
card magnets

✧ Letterheads and compliment slips: letterheads, letterhead, letter
paper, notepaper, personalised stationery, personalized stationery, personalised stationary, personalized stationary, personalised notepaper, personalized notepaper, custom notepaper,
customized notepaper, postcard, postcards, compliments slips,
personalized compliment slips

✧ Leaflets and flyers: Leaflet, leaflets, flyers, brochures, brochure,
brochure design, flyer design, flyer, presentation folders,
newsletters, sales data sheets, folders, promotional material

✧ Address stamps and labels: address labels, address label, label,
stickers, address stickers, return address labels, custom labels,
address stamp, caricature address labels

✧ Printing: business printers, printing, online design, online printing, online print ordering, online printers, online print order,
affordable printing, printing company, printing company Idaho,
printing company Boise, printing supplies, printers services,
cheap printer, cheap printing, online printer, printing online, digital printing, screen printing, offset printing, custom printing,
best printing, printing gift certificates, printing coupons, order
printing online, low priced printing, short print runs

✧ Other: advertising film, advertising lettering, book printers,
greeting cards, invitation cards, wedding cards, tshirt, tshirts,
t shirt, t-shirt, stamp, online creation, online graphics, online
design, folding paper, book, books, pdf, copyshop, annual
report, magnets, folded cards, note cards, press kit

You will note that grouping keywords and keyphrases into categories is a useful exercise, as it begins to lay the foundations for
determining your page structure and navigation later on.

Identifying related keywords

Related keyphrases and keywords have a similar meaning or inference to your main keyphrases and keywords. There is reliable empirical evidence that Google and other search engines make increasing use of semantics in assessing the quality of a page for ranking purposes. A low-quality web page, designed by spammers for search engine, rather than human, consumption, will typically be crammed full of the same search phrase, repeated over and over again. It won't contain the related words.

A high-quality page (naturally written) will, by contrast, typically be full of words semantically related to the main search term used. As search engines move ever further toward employing semantic intelligence in their ranking systems, using related keywords will become ever more important to avoid scoring low in the rankings.

Perhaps more importantly, you should remember that the phrases you might use to search for something will not be the same phrases that someone else would naturally use, so some research is required.

FORUM TOOLS There is an excellent tool on the web for locating related keywords, the GoRank Ontology Finder (Related Keywords Lookup Tool). This tool runs a "related word" enquiry against the Google index. See www.gorank.com/seotools/ontology/. Visit the forum (www.seo-expert-services.co.uk) for more excellent tools like these.

Try using an ontology tool (and an ordinary thesaurus) to identify some related terms. Your optimization campaign should ideally use a mixture of these words in both on-page and off-page activities.

Brad wants to explore related words for his important qualifying words "cheap" and "quality." He uses both the GoRank Ontology Finder and Microsoft Word's Thesaurus function and finds the following:

✧ <u>Cheap</u>: buy, cheap, discount, low cost, low priced, last minute, cheapest, bargain, cheaper, inexpensive, economical, affordable, cut-price, budget, reduced, inexpensive, on sale

✧ <u>Quality</u>: luxury, superior, class, value, five star, luxurious, high, highest

He adds suitable combinations of his main keywords and these qualifying words to the keywords list on his spreadsheet.

Often the words you find through an ontological check will actually be used more frequently by searchers than the ones you had originally selected.

Consider Doug Chalmers, purveyor of fine antiques in Windsor, UK. Doug specializes in "Victorian furnishings," so (before reading this book) he was very set on ranking well for that particular keyphrase. However, a full related-word check revealed many alternatives – including old, classic, antique, furniture, vintage, rare, Victorian, antiques, and collectible – with "antique furniture" being the most attractive choice. Without an ontological check, he could have wasted a great deal of time and energy on too narrow a selection.

Long-tail analysis

<u>Long-tail</u> keyphrases are typically related to your main strategic keywords and generally include three, four, or more words. For example, "web hosting linux," "cheap web hosting," and "web hosting control panel" might be typical long-tail phrases for a web-design business. Such phrases are known as long tail because the frequency with which they are searched on reduces as the length of the phrase increases (in a long tail that tends toward zero searches).

In the next chapter, on keyword attractiveness, I will show you how to assess the degree of popularity and competitiveness attached to each keyword and keyphrase. However, before we get there I can give you a sneak preview: Generally, the longer a phrase is, the more attractive it is, in relative terms. Here is a typical long-tail graph:

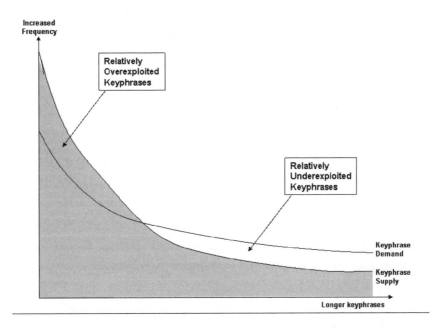

Long-tail analysis seeks to identify, for your most common keyword categories (or "stems"), the phrases that pay where demand is relatively high but competition relatively weak; what I call relatively underexploited keyphrases.

As an example, consider Sam Larder, owner of a luxury, ski-in–ski-out chalet in Verbier, Switzerland. Sam has been spending a fortune on a paid advertising campaign, selecting phrases such as "ski chalet" and "chalet verbier." Given the popularity of the resort (and the number of competing accommodation providers) he has had to pay more and more to acquire his visitors. However, after reading this book, Sam thoroughly considers his business proposition and looks at the long tail in the light of this.

Nearly all of Sam's customers have one big thing in common: They bring their children skiing with them. This might have something to do with the fact that Sam's chalet is right next door to the local crèche. He reconsiders his keyword selection and (from ontological analysis) goes for "ski chalet crèche," "ski chalet child care," "ski chalet nursery," and "ski chalet ski school." It may not surprise you to learn that Sam more than doubled his customer conversions while almost halving his costs!

I will return to phrases that pay in the next section. However, at this point all you need to understand is that it is a good idea to have several keyword chains (that link two, three, or even four keywords together) in your optimization ingredients.

Returning to the Abakus Keyword Tool (or using your SEO software), it is now time to analyze your competitors' sites more deeply. This time you are looking for the most commonly repeated two-, three-, and four-word keyphrases in the page text. Add these to your spreadsheet, again in Column A. Repeat the task for different sites and for different pages within the same site. You are aiming for a list of approximately 100 keywords and keyphrases at this stage.

> Brad investigates his competitors' sites again (only this time going down much further in the rankings and trying many different searches). He settles on a group of multi-word phrases that appear most often on competing sites, of which the following are just a few examples:
>
> ✧ <u>Two-word phrases</u>: business cards, letterhead printing, compliment slips, printed labels, address labels, print design
> ✧ <u>Three-word phrases</u>: quality business cards, business card printing, business card design, laminated business cards, letterhead stationery printing, online printing letterheads, avery address labels, printed address labels, sticky address labels, design brochures leaflets, full color printing, business brochures flyers, business printing services, online business printing, business brochure printing
> ✧ <u>Four-word phrases</u>: online business card printing, business card printing services, business card printing service, business form

printing services, cheap business card printing, business card printing company, custom business card printing, business card design printing, business card discount printing, business card printing Idaho, business card printing Boise

Brad was interested to note that "business cards" appeared more often than "business card." He has learnt another key lesson: Always pluralize your keywords where you can. You will achieve higher traffic this way, because of the way search engines handle queries and users perform searches. As I have said, learn from your competitors where you can!

For a typical small (10-page) site, you should now have approximately 35–40 one-word and two-word phrases and perhaps as many as 60–75 three-word and four-or-more-word combinations.

1.3 Keyword attractiveness

You may be wondering at this point how you are going to optimize your site for more than 100 keyphrases. Well, stop worrying! We are now going to narrow down the target list substantially in the second D–A–D step, keyword attractiveness.

Keyword attractiveness is all about balancing the demand for your chosen keywords against the number of competing sites supplying relevant results. Attractive keyphrases are those that are relatively under-exploited – these are the phrases that pay.

Imagine that SEO is like target practice, where you only have a certain amount of ammunition. There are several different targets you can shoot at, all at varying distances away from your gun sites. You are seeking bullseyes. Would you shoot at only one target, putting hole after hole through the bullseye? No! Would you aim at the targets furthest away from you and see round after round expended fruitlessly?

No! This analogy is in fact very apposite, as SEO is a very similar challenge.

You may think that you have an unlimited number of bullets. After all, you could create as many pages as there are variants in search terms and build as many links as the web will support. However, in practice you are limited by your own time, the tolerance of your customers, and the Google spam filters. Your time is probably better spent running your business than sitting at your computer doing SEO into the small hours (that's what people like me are for). Your customers are also unlikely to be impressed by hundreds of similar pages. Finally, Google does look actively for – and deflate the ranking of – sites with an excessive number of inbound links (links from other sites) relative to their traffic, or for time periods where the links to a site have grown much more quickly than one would naturally expect.

So choose your targets carefully. Make sure you take the easier bullseyes on offer (where the target is close by). Similarly, spread your effort across a wide range of targets. Finally, do not give up on the far-away targets, but be mindful of how much ammunition you are using on them. Keyword attractiveness is the toolset you use to decide where to fire – and how often.

Keyword popularity (P)

The first component of keyword attractiveness is popularity. What are the keywords most customers will use today to find your site? You may think you know already (and possibly you do), but then again you may be surprised.

One of the most wonderful things about search engines is that they make available (for public research purposes) "insider data" about what people search for on their sites. They do this in a variety of ways, generally through application program interfaces (APIs), which allow developers to point their web-based or desktop software directly at the underlying search engine index.

Imagine that: basically the highest-quality market research data that has ever been made available, continually refreshed in real time and based on massive sample sizes. Wouldn't you be mad not to take advantage of this data? Of course, and I am going to show you how.

To access the industry data yourself, you basically have two choices. Either you purchase SEO software that directly interacts with industry data sources; or you make use of the (now relatively limited) free keyword-analysis tools online.

| FORUM |
| TOOLS |

On the forum (www.seo-expert-services.co.uk), I maintain a comprehensive and up-to-date list of all the most important SEO tools and software, including those appropriate for keyword-popularity research. Via the forum, you can obtain a special discounted price on the software I most frequently use.

However, for the purposes of this section, I will work with the current best free resource: www.digitalpoint.com/tools/suggestion/. The Digital Point tool allows you to check for recent combinations of search words (and their derivatives) on the search engines, returning search frequencies for each. The data you will be accessing is for the most recently completed calendar month.

Bear this in mind if your business is seasonal in nature. For example, if you sell Halloween costumes, you are likely to get an inflated view of search rates if you undertake this analysis in November and thus work on the October data!

Visit the tool and try entering some of the two-, three-, and four-word combinations on your keyword list. Make a note of the resulting frequencies. You will notice that you can drill down from phrases into their subcategories (by clicking on a phrase in the results).

Brad finds that the main subcategory for "business printing" (6,245 results) is "business card printing" (19,254 results). This surprises him more than perhaps it should. More than 50% of all US businesses are now home based, so the SOHO/B2C part of his market is bigger than he could ever have imagined. Consumers, not

companies, are what drives big search popularity numbers, and
most bedroom entrepreneurs need business cards.

You should really multiply the Digital Point search numbers returned by
approximately 2.5 (which extrapolates its numbers to a rough estimate
of worldwide searches). You can then add these numbers to your spreadsheet (in Column B) to give you the top keywords and phrases for your
business, based on popularity alone.

You will find, as did Brad, that clicking up and down through the
Digital Point results will suggest many more keyword combinations that
your competitors have not spotted. Brad, for example, found that "color
business card printing" and even "full color business card printing" were
quite popular, despite not featuring on his competitors' sites. Add all of
these new finds to your keyword list in Column A and aim to get your
total up to about 150 different keywords and keyphrases.

Keyword competitiveness (C)

To know the popularity of keywords is really less than half the battle, however. It is vital to know what you are up against: If you are entering a very
competitive marketplace (where there are millions of sites using exactly
your keywords), it will be a long and hard slog to get up there with the
very best. Don't pick the targets that are miles away from your gun sites!

Keyword competitiveness is extracted from the number of results
returned from a Google search on the search terms concerned. For
example, a search on business cards returns, at the time of writing,
around 245 million results.

Return to your spreadsheet and look at Column C, raw competition. Perform a search on Google for each of your listed keyphrases in
turn and enter the number of results into your spreadsheet. Once you've
done this, a numerical sort of Column C gives you, in ranking order, the
most competitive raw search terms related to your business, products,
and services.

Directly competing sites (Column D) are those that have the exact keyword phrase you are analyzing in the <u>anchor text</u> (the text the user clicks) of links to their site from other websites (rather than simply having the words in that phrase on their pages). Directly competing sites are your serious competition: They are likely already to have invested time and energy into search engine optimization campaigns. They are also likely to continue doing so in the future.

To work out D for any search phrase, I use the <u>allinanchor:</u> Google operator. For example, a search on "allinanchor:business cards" returns 365,000 results and "allinanchor:online business card printing" returns just 13,300. Brad is beginning to smile at last – suddenly the odds don't look quite so daunting.

Perform an allinanchor: search on Google for each term in turn and enter the number of results into your spreadsheet in Column D. A numerical sort of the column gives you, in ranking order, a better idea of the truly competitive search terms related to your business, products, and services. By now, your spreadsheet should look something like this early draft of Brad's:

Keywords	Monthly searches	Raw competition	Directly competing	KEI	KOI
Business cards	214,349	245,000,000	365,000		
Business card printing	19,524	42,100,000	36,600		
Online business card printing	1,265	516,000,000	13,300		

FORUM TOOLS

To speed up your extraction of Google search results numbers, you may wish to make use of another neat tool, the Google Smackdown analyzer at www.onfocus.com/googlesmack/

down.asp, which allows you to compare the overall frequency of two competing keyword sets across the whole of Google's results.

Keyword opportunity index (KOI)

The keyword effectiveness index (KEI), first popularized by Sumantra Roy, is a way of combining keyword popularity (P) with raw keyword competitiveness (C) to give a composite score. The usual formula for KEI is popularity squared, divided by the number of competing sites using that keyword. This gives a higher significance to the popularity measure (which is the right way to look at it).

The KEI measure is often used to rank the effectiveness of different keyword combinations. In your spreadsheet, use Column E (entitled KEI) to calculate the keyword effectiveness of each phrase. The formula in each cell should be $P\wedge2/C$.

I have developed my own attractiveness measure, the keyword opportunity index (KOI), which takes Sumantra's work a step further and is a more sophisticated measure of the opportunity presented by each keyword. KOI is calculated as $KOI = (P\wedge2/D)$ and thus bases the attractiveness of a keyword or keyphrase solely on directly competing sites.

Enter the formula $P\wedge2/D$ into each Column F cell of your spreadsheet to calculate KOI. A numerical sort on Column F gives you, in ranking order, a composite rating of the attractiveness of each keyword for an SEO campaign on your business, products, and services. It is this KOI number that I refer to most during the on-page and off-page optimization phases to follow.

> Brad's final keyword analysis spreadsheet contains a staggering 570 phrases. However, for the purposes of illustration I will continue to focus just on the business card category of his analysis. Opposite is a short extract from the finished product.

Keywords	Monthly searches	Raw competition	Directly competing	KEI	KOI
Business cards	214,349	245,000,000	365,000	187.53	125,878.07
Business card printing	19,524	42,100,000	36,600	9.05	10,414.93
Business printing	6,345	127,000,000	120,000	0.32	335.49
Online business card printing	1,265	516,000,000	13,300	0.00	120.32
Business card printing services	934	256,000,000	11,800	0.00	73.73
Business card printing service	811	234,000,000	10,400	0.00	63.24
Color business card printing	793	98,500,000	12,300	0.01	51.13
Full color business card printing	426	2,630,000	774	0.07	234.47
Cheap business card printing	215	35,000,000	736	0.00	62.81
Business card printing company	179	82,700,000	10,100	0.00	3.17

Brad is delighted with the results. He finds, to his surprise, that the market for online business cards is relatively uncompetitive, with fewer than 400,000 competing pages, chasing 214,000 daily searches. His long-tailed demand curve falls steeply but the competition curve is flat, meaning that Brad has lots of opportunities to make money.

Note the phrase "full color business card printing." Like our earlier "ski chalet child care" illustration, this is a great example of a phrase that pays. With fewer than 800 competing pages, I share Brad's confidence that he can achieve a #1 ranking on Google for a search term that more than 400 people search for each and every day. Note, also, how much more effective the KOI comparison is than the KEI score. Would Brad have unearthed the "full color business card printing" phrase without using KOI?

At this point, it is worth injecting a note of caution. Digital Point numbers are extrapolated from a relatively small sample of searches. As such, any search frequency of less than 1,000 can be unreliable. It may be worth running your full analysis over a period of three month ends just to be sure than some overenthusiastic searchers have not skewed the results.

Prioritizing your raw list

It will not have escaped your notice that by now, you may have a very long list indeed of keyphrase candidates for your site. Brad, as I have noted, has over 500 at this point. However, candidates are all they are. Unless you have a very large, content-rich site, it is unlikely that you will need so many phrases. Nor is it likely that you would be able to optimize effectively for so many.

Can I suggest that at this point, you cull a full 50% of your entire list, based on a KOI sort. Then add back in 10–15% of the words with the highest search frequencies. This should give you a more workable database with which to enter the final part of the D-A-D method, keyword deployment.

1.4 Keyword deployment

Before you begin to use your keywords for real, it is important to narrow down your long list of keyphrases yet further; to use them more efficiently in combination with one another; and to ensure that the end result is not unreadable garbage. In short, you need to understand the basic rules of what I call <u>keyword deployment</u>.

Whether you are building links, choosing domain names. or writing page text, you are trying to include your keywords in all of these in a search-engine-friendly way. While different search engines use slightly different algorithms, they all place importance on prominence, proximity, and density, the three basic rules of keyword deployment.

Follow the simple rules in this section in moderation and you will always get a good result. Overdo any one and you risk getting flagged as spam. The acid test is: Does it still read well for the human user? If it does and obeys the three basic rules, then the search-engine spiders (robot browsers, also known as crawlers, or Googlebots on Google) will love you. If, alternatively, your keyword stuffing would make a user laugh (or cry), then you are running a very real risk of failure.

All the world's a text block

First, it is important to understand that spiders love text. Every piece of information about a page can be turned into a long list of words. The domain name (the name of your site), the URL (the web address, technically the uniform resource locator), the filename (from which you created the page), and the page title are all text blocks. So too are the page meta tags (elements in the programming that provide information about the page), heading tags, page text, and even the alt tags on images (which describe what the image is, for spiders or the visually impaired). Finally, the links to and away from each page are text blocks. Google goes even further and looks at all the text blocks of all the pages that link to (or are linked from) your page. In short, all the world is a text block to a Googlebot.

So if you read on a forum somewhere that "domain names don't matter" or "alt tags are overrated," ignore that. As I have said, SEO is like throwing mud at a wall – every bit you throw will stick to some extent and the more mud you throw, the more will stick. You can afford to ignore no text block in your quest for dominance!

Each text block has a beginning, an end, and a pattern in the middle. Google will examine each text block separately and take it into the index for that page. Try experimenting on a search using the intitle:anykeyword and inurl:anykeyword operators (search for intitle:antiques or inurl:antiques, for example) and you will see that Google finds a separate place (and weighting) in its index for every text block. In evaluating each block, Google will assume that relevant keywords appear earlier in each text block; tend to appear together; and tend to appear often. Put simply, the spider is looking for prominence, proximity, and density.

Keyword prominence

All search engines attempt to determine the most important words on a page, in a tag, or in a link. In the absence of any guidance from your HTML (see below), the first and most important measure used is that of prominence (i.e., the closer a word is to the front of the analyzed text area, the more relevant or important it is).

Prominence implies that a word used at the beginning of a link or piece of text is more important than the rest. The words that follow are scored lower and lower by the algorithm until (in a very long text section) their value tends toward zero or is cut off by a programmatic truncation.

As an example, consider these two alternative page titles:

✧ Chambers Print LLC – we offer printing services to businesses
✧ Business Printing Services – from Chambers Print LLC

Now you understand prominence, you will appreciate that, all other things being equal, the second of these alternative titles will produce better search engine rankings (for "business printing" or "printing services") than the first option can.

Remember that search engines evaluate each important page area or inbound link separately. As such, the title tag, meta-description tag, keyword tag, heading tags, alt text tags, and page text all produce their own prominence pictures that, together, tell the search engine a great deal about your page.

This is one of many reasons not using standard HTML mark-ups is simply a wasted opportunity. For example, if you break up your text with subheadings (all of which use the <h1> tag), the search engine will attach a prominence value to the first words of each of these in turn. More on this later in the on-page optimization section (page 97).

Keyword proximity

The next factor used by search engines to determine keyword importance (or relevance) is proximity. Keyword proximity refers to how close the keywords that make up your keyphrase are to each other.

As an example, consider these two alternative headings:

✧ Printing Business Cards & Letterheads
✧ Business Card Printing & Letterhead Printing

While the first option is perhaps more elegant English, the second will produce better rankings for a page optimized on either "business card printing" or "letterhead printing," as the relevant words appear next to one another and in the correct order.

In short, you should always endeavor to keep your keywords together as a unit. Where this is not possible (i.e., the text would not read well for a human user), do your best to keep them not too far away from each other. For example, "business card and letterhead printing" is still an improvement on "business card and letterhead stationery and printing services."

The reason proximity works is that search engines are machines that follow ruthless logic. If someone searches on "letterhead printing" then logic dictates that pages full of the text "letterhead printing" – or linked with the anchor text "letterhead printing" – are more likely to be relevant to the searcher than pages that do not exhibit this characteristic.

Keyword density

The final keyword deployment factor used by search engines to determine keyword importance is <u>density</u>. This can be defined as the relative frequency with which a keyword or phrase is found within the page text area being examined (whether this is a title, heading, link anchor text, or page text). "Relative" in this context means relative to all the other words in the text area.

In other words, density is calculated as the number of words in the keyphrase multiplied by the frequency with which they occur together, and divided by the total number of words (including the keyword).

As an example, consider these two alternative headings:

⬦ Business Printing
⬦ Business Printing and more

While both options score equally on prominence and proximity, the first wins on the density criterion. Here keyword density is at 100% (for the phrase "business printing") compared to just 50% for option 2.

Many webmasters use titles or descriptions that include words or phrases like "and more" or "world's biggest selection of." I call these phrases redundant text, in that they have no SEO value and serve only to dilute the effectiveness of your page copy. Get rid of them where you can.

There are thus two ways to improve density: either increase the frequency with which certain phrases are used or reduce the overall number of words in the text area. Again, moderation is key here. Too high a density for the type of content involved can trigger a spam penalty from Google.

In the on-page and off-page sections (pages 97 and 132) I explore keyword density in much greater detail, including the ideal density for each text area to score well in search engines while avoiding spam triggers.

Keyword splitting

I said there were three rules, didn't I? Well, actually there are five. The first of my additional rules is keyword splitting. It cannot have escaped your notice above that having business cards and letterheads together on one page inherently dilutes the prominence, proximity, and density of both products.

If Brad had a separate page for each of his two products, then he could reduce the stem for each to just two words, then add related keyphrases to build density. So, using the title tag as an example:

✧ Page 1: Business Card Printing – Online Business Card Design & Printing Services
✧ Page 2: Letterhead Printing – Online Letterhead Design & Printing Services

But why stop here? Brad could actually create a section for each product, then have individual pages for each aspect of the service. So why not:

✧ Section 1: Business Card Printing
• Page 1.1: Business Card Printing > Online Business Card Design Services

- Page 1.2: Business Card Printing > Online Business Card Printing Services
- Page 1.3: Business Card Printing > Luxury Business Cards

Etc,

As you can see, this begins to lead us into site structure and navigational optimization (which there is a section on later, see page 86) but at this point, all you need to understand is that splitting out keyphrase categories into separate pages and sections helps with the three main principles of prominence, proximity, and density.

Keyword splicing

The second of my additional rules is keyword <u>splicing</u>. The observant among you might have noticed that Brad managed to hit two birds with one stone in the example above. From his original keyword analysis he had:

- ◇ Online Business Card Printing – 1,265 daily searches
- ◇ Business Card Printing Services – 934 daily searches

By deploying the phrase "online business card printing services" as a five-keyword chain, Brad actually managed to include two proximate three-word keyphrases in one longer, composite phrase. You should look for the same keyword-splicing opportunities in your keyword deployment planning.

Weighting your deployment

You should now split your prioritized raw list of keywords into three groups: A, B, and C. Your A list will include suitable candidates for homepage content and product or service sections and categories. Your B list will contain the individual products and services themselves; and your C list will incorporate other attractive phrases and qualifying categories (which may or may not have individual pages to themselves).

For example, Brad would go for:

A list
1 Business card printing
2 Letterhead printing

B list
1.1 Online business card custom design
1.2 Online business card custom printing
1.3 Online business card ordering

C list
1.1.1 Quality business card designs
Include variations: luxury, value, superior, 5 star, highest
1.1.2 Cheap business card designs
Include variations: discount, low cost, bargain, affordable, etc.

This is just an extract from Brad's planning, but gives you an idea of how to break down your keyphrases into workable categories and lists that you can more readily deploy later.

You should select, as far as possible, the most attractive phrases (as measured by KOI) in your A list, the next most attractive in your B list, and the least most attractive in your C list. This will normally follow, as most people tend to search more often on broad category matches than individual products.

Use common sense, however, as it is unlikely that KOI alone will give you a sensible list. If in doubt, always promote the phrases with higher search popularity. Remember that a sound business is never built wholly on niches.

Site-wide and deep phrases

To complete the keyword deployment phase, look again at your A list. Try to identify 3–5 two-word and 4–6 three-word phrases that have the highest keyword weighting. These phrases will become <u>site-wide</u> phrases; the rest will be <u>deep</u> phrases. Site-wide phrases will be used to optimize your homepage and liberally sprinkled throughout the rest of the site. Deep phrases will typically be confined only to individual sections, categories, or content pages.

Now you are fully ready and properly equipped to embark on your journey of search engine optimization.

Step 2: Courting the crawl

If you picked up a book on SEO from two or three years ago, there would have probably been a whole chapter on search engine submission. There were also businesses that used to specialize in this activity alone. One or two of them still vainly pursue this business model, but I am afraid the world has moved on. The modern way to handle Google inclusion is through the use of sitemaps (see later in this step) and a well-structured site.

Courting the crawl is all about helping Google to find your site and, most importantly, to index all your pages properly. It may surprise you, but even many well-established big names (with huge sites) have very substantial problems in this area. In fact, the bigger the client the more time I typically need to spend focused on the crawl.

As you will see, good websites are hosted well, set up properly, and, above all, structured sensibly. Whether you are working on a new site or reworking an existing internet presence, I will show you how to be found by Google and have all your pages included fully in the Google search index.

2.1 How Google finds sites and pages

All major search engines use spider programs (also known as crawlers or robots) to scour the web, collect documents, give each a unique reference, scan their text, and hand them off to an indexing program. Where the scan picks up hyperlinks to other documents, those documents are then fetched in their turn. Google's spider is called Googlebot and you can see it hitting your site if you look at your web logs. A typical Googlebot entry (in the browser section of your logs) might look like this:

Mozilla/5.0 (compatible; Googlebot/2.1; http://www.google.com/bot.html)

How Googlebot first finds your site

There are essentially four ways in which Googlebot finds your new site. The first and most obvious way is for you to submit your URL to Google for crawling, via the "Add URL" form at www.google.com/addurl.html. The second way is when Google finds a link to your site from another site that it has already indexed and subsequently sends its spider to follow the link. The third way is when you sign up for Google Webmaster Tools (more on this on page 228), verify your site, and submit a sitemap. The fourth (and final) way is when you redirect an already indexed webpage to the new page (for example using a 301 redirect, about which there is more later).

In the past you could use search engine submission software, but Google now prevents this – and prevents spammers bombarding it with new sites – by using a CAPTCHA, a challenge-response test to determine whether the user is human, on its Add URL page. CAPTCHA stands for Completely Automated Public Turing test to tell Computers and Humans Apart, and typically takes the form of a distorted image of letters and/or numbers that you have to type in as part of the submission.

How quickly you can expect to be crawled

There are no firm guarantees as to how quickly new sites – or pages – will be crawled by Google and then appear in the search index. However, following one of the four actions above, you would normally expect to be crawled within a month and then see your pages appear in the index two to three weeks afterwards. In my experience, submission via Google Webmaster Tools is the most effective way to manage your crawl and to be crawled quickly, so I typically do this for all my clients.

What Googlebot does on your site

Once Googlebot is on your site, it crawls each page in turn. When it finds an internal link, it will remember it and crawl it, either later that visit or on a subsequent trip to your site. Eventually, Google will crawl your whole site.

In the next step (priming your pages, page 92) I will explain how Google indexes your pages for retrieval during a search query. In the step after that (landing the links, page 128) I will explain how each indexed page is actually ranked. However, for now the best analogy I can give you is to imagine that your site is a tree, with the base of the trunk being your home page, your directories the branches, and your pages the leaves on the end of the branches. Google will crawl up the tree like nutrients from the roots, gifting each part of the tree with its all-important PageRank. If your tree is well structured and has good symmetry, the crawl will be even and each branch and leaf will enjoy a proportionate benefit. There is (much) more on this later.

Controlling Googlebot

For some webmasters Google crawls too often (and consumes too much bandwidth). For others it visits too infrequently. Some complain that it doesn't visit their entire site and others get upset when areas that they didn't want accessible via search engines appear in the Google index.

To a certain extent, it is not possible to *attract* robots. Google will visit your site often if the site has excellent content that is updated frequently and cited often by other sites. No amount of shouting will make you popular! However, it is certainly possible to *deter* robots. You can control both the pages that Googlebot crawls and (should you wish) request a reduction in the frequency or depth of each crawl.

To prevent Google from crawling certain pages, the best method is to use a robots.txt file. This is simply an ASCII text file that you place at the root of your domain. For example, if your domain is

http://www.yourdomain.com, place the file at http://www.yourdomain.
com/robots.txt. You might use robots.txt to prevent Google indexing
your images, running your PERL scripts (for example, any forms for
your customers to fill in), or accessing pages that are copyrighted. Each
block of the robots.txt file lists first the name of the spider, then the list
of directories or files it is not allowed to access on subsequent, separate
lines. The format supports the use of wildcard characters, such as * or
? to represent numbers or letters.

The following robots.txt file would prevent all robots from accessing your image or PERL script directories and just Googlebot from
accessing your copyrighted material and copyright notice page (assuming you had placed images in an "images" directory and your copyrighted material in a "copyright" directory):

```
User-agent: *
Disallow: /images/
Disallow: /cgi-bin/
```

```
User-agent: Googlebot
Disallow: /copyright/
Disallow: /content/copyright-notice.html
```

To control Googlebot's crawl rate, you need to sign up for Google
Webmaster Tools (a process I cover in detail in the section on tracking
and tuning, page 228). You can then choose from one of three settings
for your crawl: faster, normal, or slower (although sometimes faster is
not an available choice). Normal is the default (and recommended)
crawl rate. A slower crawl will reduce Googlebot's traffic on your server,
but Google may not be able to crawl your site as often.

You should note that none of these crawl adjustment methods is
100% reliable (particularly for spiders that are less well behaved than
Googlebot). Even less likely to work are metadata robot instructions,
which you incorporate in the meta tags section of your web page.

However, I will include them for completeness. The meta tag to stop spiders indexing a page is:

<meta name="robots" content="NOINDEX">

The meta tag to prevent spiders following the links on your page is:

<meta name="robots" content="NOFOLLOW">

Google is known to observe both the NOINDEX and NOFOLLOW instructions, but as other search engines often do not, I would recommend the use of robots.txt as a better method.

Sitemaps

A sitemap (with which you may well be familiar) is an HTML page containing an ordered list of all the pages on your site (or, for a large site, at least the most important pages).

Good sitemaps help humans to find what they are looking for and help search engines to orient themselves and manage their crawl activities. Googlebot, in particular, may complete the indexing of your site over multiple visits, and even after that will return from time to time to check for changes. A sitemap gives the spider a rapid guide to the structure of your site and what has changed since last time.

Googlebot will also look at the number of levels – and breadth – of your sitemap (together with other factors) to work out how to distribute your PageRank, the numerical weighting it assigns to the relative importance of your pages.

Creating your sitemap

Some hosting providers (for example 1and1) provide utilities via their web control panel to create your sitemap, so you should always check

with your provider first. If this service is not available, then visit
www.xml-sitemaps.com and enter your site URL into the generator box.
After the program has generated your sitemap, click the relevant link to
save the XML file output (XML stands for eXtensible Markup
Language and is more advanced than HTML) so that you can store the
file on your computer. You might also pick up the HTML version for use
on your actual site. Open the resulting file with a text editor such as
Notepad and take a look through it.

At the very beginning of his web redevelopment, Brad creates just
two pages, the Chambers Print homepage and a Contact us page.
He uses a sitemap-generator tool to automatically create a sitemap,
then edits the file manually to tweak the priority tags (see below)
and add a single office location in a KML file (see also below):

```
<?xml version="1.0" encoding="UTF-8" ?>
<urlset xmlns="http://www.sitemaps.org/schemas/sitemap/0.9"
xmlns:xsi="http://www.w3.org/2001/XMLSchema-instance"
xsi:schemaLocation="http://www.sitemaps.org/schemas/sitemap/0.
9 http://www.sitemaps.org/schemas/sitemap/0.9/sitemap.xsd">
  <url>
    <loc>http://www.chambersprint.com/</loc>
    <priority>0.9</priority>
    <lastmod>2007-07-12T20:05:17+00:00</lastmod>
    <changefreq>daily</changefreq>
  </url>
  <url>
    <loc>http://www.chambersprint.com/about-us/contact-
us.html</loc>
    <priority>0.8</priority>
    <lastmod>2007-07-12T20:05:17+00:00</lastmod>
    <changefreq>daily</changefreq>
  </url>
```

```
<url>
  <loc>http://www.chambersprint.com/about-us/chambers-boise-
branch.kml</loc>
  </url>
</urlset>
```

I cover KML in greater detail later (under local optimization, page 217) so all you need to understand for now is that a KML file tells Google where something is located (longitude and latitude) – in this case, Chambers' Boise branch.

Sitemaps.org defines the standard protocol. There are four compulsory elements. The sitemap must:

✧ Begin with an opening <urlset> tag and end with a closing </urlset> tag.
✧ Specify the namespace within the <urlset> tag. The namespace is the protocol or set of rules you are using and its URL is preceded by "xmlns" to indicate it is an XML namespace.
✧ Include a <url> entry for each URL, as a parent XML tag (the top level or trunk in your site's "family tree").
✧ Include a <loc> child entry for each <url> parent tag (at least one branch for each trunk).

All other tags are optional and support for them varies among search engines. At https://www.google.com/webmasters/tools/docs/en/protocol.html, Google explains how it interprets sitemaps.

You will note that Brad used the following optional tags:

✧ The <priority> tag gives Google a hint as to the importance of a URL relative to other URLs in your sitemap. Valid values range from 0.0 to 1.0. The default priority (i.e., if no tag is present) is inferred to be 0.5.

❖ The <u>lastmod</u> tag defines the date on which the file was last modified and is in W3C Datetime format, for example YYYY-MM-DDThh:mm:ss for year, month, day, and time in hours, minutes and seconds. This format allows you to omit the time portion, if desired, and just use YYYY-MM-DD.

❖ The <u>changefreq</u> tag defines how frequently the page is likely to change. Again, this tag merely provides a hint to spiders and Googlebot may chose to ignore it altogether. Valid values are always, hourly, daily, weekly, monthly, yearly, never. The value "always" should be used to describe documents that change each time they are accessed. The value "never" should be used to describe archived URLs.

My advice with respect to the use of optional tags is as follows:

❖ *Do* use the <priority> tag. Set a value of 0.9 for the homepage, 0.8 for section pages, 0.7 for category pages, and 0.6 for important content pages (e.g., landing pages and money pages). For less important content pages, use a setting of 0.3. For archived content pages, use 0.2. Try to achieve an overall average across all pages of near to 0.5.

❖ Only use the <lastmod> tag for pages that from part of a blog or a news/press-release section. Even then, do not bother adding the time stamp. So <lastmod>2008-07-12</lastmod> is fine.

❖ Adding a <changefreq> tag is unlikely to help you, as Google will probably ignore it anyway (particularly if your pages demonstrably are not updated as frequently as your sitemap claims).

FORUM TOOLS If you do make manual changes to an XML file that has been automatically generated for you, you may wish to visit a sitemap XML validator to check its correct formation prior to moving on to referencing and submission. On the forum (www.seo-expert-services.co.uk) I maintain an up-to-date list. My current favourite is the XML Sitemaps validator, at www.xml-sitemaps.com/validate-xml-sitemap.html.

Referencing your sitemap

Before we turn to submission (i.e., actively notifying the search engines of your sitemap), I would like to briefly explore passive notification, which I call sitemap referencing.

SiteMaps.org (to which all the major engines now subscribe) sets a standard for referencing that utilizes the very same robots.txt file I explained to you above (page 57). When a spider visits your site and reads your robots.txt file, you can now tell it where to find your sitemap. For example (where your sitemap file is called sitemap.xml and is located in the root of your website):

```
User-agent: *
Sitemap: http://www.yourdomain.com/sitemap.xml
Disallow: /cgi-bin/
Disallow: /assets/images/
```

The example robots.txt file tells the crawler how to find your sitemap and not to crawl either your cgi-bin directory (containing PERL scripts not intended for the human reader) or your images directory (to save bandwidth). For more information on the robots.txt standard, you can refer to the authoritative website www.robotstxt.org.

Submitting your sitemap

Now we turn to the active submission of your site map to the major search engines (the modern equivalent of old-fashioned search engine submission). Over time, all the search engines will move toward the Sitemaps.org standard for submission, which is to use a ping URL submission syntax. Basically this means you give your sitemap address to the search engine and request it to send out a short burst of data and "listen" for a reply, like the echo on a submarine sonar search.

At time of writing, I only recommend using this method for Ask.com. Amend the following to add the full URL path to your sitemap file, copy it into your browser URL bar, and hit return:

http://submissions.ask.com/ping?sitemap=http://www.yourdomain.com /sitemap.xml

Ask.com will present you with a reassuring confirmation page, then crawl your sitemap file shortly thereafter.

MSN has yet to implement a formal interface for sitemap submission. To monitor the situation, visit the LiveSearch official blog (at http://blogs.msdn.com/livesearch) where future improvements are likely to be communicated. However, for the time being I recommend undertaking two steps to ensure that MSN indexes your site:

- ✦ Reference your sitemap in your robots.txt file (see above).
- ✦ Ping Moreover using http://api.moreover.com/ping?u=http:// yourdomain.com/yoursitemap.xml.

Moreover.com is the official provider of RSS feeds to the myMSN portal, so I always work on the (probably erroneous) theory that submission to Moreover may somehow feed into the main MSN index somewhere down the track. (RSS is sometimes called Really Simple Syndication and supplies "feeds" on request from a particular site, usually a news site or a blog, to a news reader on your desktop, such as Google Reader.)

Both Google (which originally developed the XML schema for sitemaps) and Yahoo! offer dedicated tools to webmasters, which include both the verification of site ownership and submission of sitemaps:

✧ Google Webmaster Tools: www.google.com/webmasters.

✧ Yahoo! Site Explorer: https://siteexplorer.search.yahoo.com.

To use Google Webmaster Tools, you must first obtain a Google account (something I cover in more detail in the section on Adwords, page 187). You then log in, click on "My Account," and follow the link to Webmaster Tools. Next, you need tell Google all the sites you own and begin the verification process. Put the URL of your site (e.g., http://www.yourdomain.com) into the Add Sites box and hit return. Google presents you with a page containing a "next step" to verify your site. Click on the Verify Site link and choose the "Add a Metatag" option. Google presents you with a unique meta tag, in the following format:

<meta name="verify-v1" content="uniquecode=" />

Edit your site and add the verification meta tag between the head tags on your homepage. Tab back to Google and click on the Verify button to complete the process. Now you can add your sitemap by clicking on the sitemap column link next to your site. Choose the "Add General SiteMap" option and complete the sitemap URL using the input box. You're all done!

Yahoo! follows a similar approach to Google on Yahoo! Site Explorer. Sign up, sign in, add a site, and click on the verification button. With Yahoo! you need to upload a verification key file (in HTML format) to the root directory of your web server. Then you can return to Site Explorer and tell Yahoo! to start authentication. This takes up to 24 hours. At the same time you can also add your sitemap by clicking on the "Manage" button and adding the sitemap as a feed.

2.2 Setting up a new site

There are two key choices to make when setting up a new website: your web host and your domain name. Many business owners give little thought to either. However, a sound house is built on good foundations and these two areas have a greater significance to SEO than you might think. If you are indeed in the happy position of reading this book prior to building a new site, this section is for you. If you are not, don't panic; this will still be useful reading and I cover existing sites in the very next section.

Choosing your host

It may surprise you that where your site is hosted has any impact at all on your search engine position. However, it is one of the most important decisions you will make – host in haste and repent at leisure.

If at any point you would like to know who is hosting a site (for example one of your competitors), simply visit the Whois lookup at www.domaintools.com and type the domain you want to check into the search bar.

Speed

First, be aware that any search engine spider contains "time-out" code that prevents it from fully indexing a site that loads too slowly. If your web pages are large and your hosting provider is slow, this could present a real barrier to your full site being indexed.

Secondly, you should note that an inadvertent leak of sections of the Google algorithm onto the web revealed that Google tracks a variable called timedout-queries_total, suggesting that the number of time-outs is itself also a factor in ranking. In other words, a site that takes ages to load (or crashes often; see below) is assumed to be a low-quality site and will thus rank poorly.

Fortunately, there is an easy way to check the speed of a site. Visit Alexa.com (a service from Amazon) and enter the homepage URL of some sample sites into the search box. Find each site in the list of results and click on the "Rank" link, then the "Overview" link. Alternatively, simply type into your web browser the URL http://www.alexa.com/data/details/main?url=yourdomain.com.

Scroll down the Overview page until you get to the Site Stats section. Under the Speed heading you will see an assessment of the speed of this site compared to all the other domains in the Alexa database (which is pretty huge). The speed statistic is a measurement of the time it takes for pages on a site to load and is based on load times experienced by Alexa Toolbar users. Load times can be affected by a number of factors, including the size in kilobytes of your web pages, the responsiveness and location of the site's servers, and the internet connection speeds of the site's typical users.

I would ideally want to see (for my customers) a site rated by Alexa as very fast. At least 80% of all sites would be slower than yours and, preferably, 90% of all sites would be slower. However, this may not be possible if the nature of your business requires very rich (and thus large) web pages that are full of formatting, pictures, and text. In this situation you should benchmark your own speed against that of your competitors' sites (again using Alexa). Ensure that you are at least 10 percentage points better than their position.

Obviously, the best way to get a lightning-fast site is to pay for a lightning-fast hosting provider. Speed is a product of the computing power at the disposal of your host and the size of its pipe onto the internet backbone (among other things). If you are looking to host on the cheap, you may be disappointed. As for automobiles, power and speed tend to come at a price. Hosting is not an area where I would cut corners.

Reliability

You will not be able to control when Googlebot and other search engine spiders visit your site. If they visit while your site is down, the aforementioned timedout-queries_total variable will tick upwards, which isn't good. Often webmasters are actually unaware of their site downtimes. Many such outages only last a matter of minutes and can happen at 3 o'clock on a Sunday morning, so neither you nor your customers may ever notice them. But Google will notice – and make its own algorithmic note.

Once you have your site up and running, there are a number of site-monitoring tools you can purchase or use for free on the web. One is the Kane Internet Seer web-monitoring tool, which sends you a regular email containing site-uptime data. Sign up at www.internetseer.com/home.

As you are still at the host-selection stage, you can compare the latest uptime data across a range of providers at the Netcraft site (www.netcraft.com). Look for providers that enjoy a consistent position in the top 10 over many months (rather than those that come and go). There are many providers that enjoy zero outages during any given month (which should be a minimum prerequisite for the serious webmaster). Even the very best, however, will have some failed requests.

Again, as for speed, when you track back top-ranked performers to their pricing packages, you may be disappointed to find that they are more expensive than you were hoping to pay. This is not surprising: Excellent performance (or so-called "high availability") requires significant infrastructure investment. The cost must be recovered from customers. If you are going to economize on anything, I would recommend you do not do this with your hosting provider, As with speed, reliability is not an area to scrimp on.

Operating system

If you're not technically minded and leave all this to your IT department, you may want to skim through this section. When you visit Netcraft you may notice that Linux (or other Unix-based servers) is overrepresented in the top-performers list when compared to FreeBSD and Windows. This has always been the case on the web – and will probably continue to be so. Don't misunderstand me: I am not a Microsoft basher and your choice of operating system will depend on more factors than simply SEO or server performance. You may, for example, like the Microsoft FrontPage software for creating your web pages. However, you can use a Linux/Unix-based server whether you have a Mac or a Windows-based PC, and the inherent stability of the Unix-based server platform is hard to ignore. Do take the operating system into account when choosing where to host.

Linux presents additional, functional attractions beyond its inherent stability. As we shall see later, a number of server-side SEO tasks are easier to achieve on Linux than on other platforms. Another advantage is that it is based on OpenSource foundations. This means that you save money on (otherwise expensive) database and other licenses. If (as I have recommended) you are spending more on speed and reliability, spending less on your system software may well prove an attractive way to keep overall costs down.

Geographical location

Did you know that the location of your provider's servers, at the time of writing, can make a big impact on your search engine rankings in local varieties of Google? I cover this in greater detail in the "making the map" section (page 204). However, a short summary now should prove informative.

If, for example, you host with landl.co.uk (one of the UK's biggest hosting providers), your servers will actually be based in its German data center. If your TLD (top-level domain) is .com (rather than .co.uk), there is a strong probability that Google will interpret your site as being German based (even if all your contact details on – and links to – the site are UK oriented). If you then go to Google.de and search on "Seiten aus Deutschland" (sites from Germany), your site will perform well in the rankings. However, you will struggle ever to rank well in "Pages from the UK" on Google.co.uk.

On the Netcraft site there is a "What's that site running" dialogue box, where you can enter a domain name and see, in the results, the country where its IP address is based. Alternatively, try http:// whois.domaintools.com/yourdomain.com and see a similarly comprehensive summary from the DomainTools site.

If you have determined a shortlist of possible hosting providers but are unclear on where they host their sites, try looking up the location of their corporate websites (as this will normally be in the same place as they host their clients). If this fails, do not be afraid to give the provider a call and ask. Its staff may be unaware of the SEO issues, but it is not unreasonable for them to know where the data center is.

There are other, more practical reasons for hosting in the country where most of your customers live: If you do so, your customers will generally have a shorter hop to your site over the web, so your pages will load more quickly and time out less often.

Flexibility

If you are planning to have more than one site, costs can stack up. It is also likely that Google will recognize your sites as being related and will ascribe less weight to any links between your related sites in determining the ranking of any one of them.

This is why some hosting providers are beginning to advertise "multiple domain hosting" (i.e., you can have more than one domain in the same package) and "separate C Block IP addresses" (i.e., Google will not so readily recognize the different domains as being related; a C

Block is a group of unique numerical addresses allocated to a hosting provider).

In my view, the related domains risk is overstated. Matt Cutts, a blogging engineer at Google (and the unofficial voice of the company), has confirmed that related sites penalties do indeed apply, as a way of tackling spammers who build multiple interlinked sites to manipulate rankings. However, he has also said that you would need to be hosting hundreds of sites together to risk being adversely affected by this.

My advice would be never to host more than 10 sites with the same hosting provider and not to worry too much about different C Blocks. If you do ever suffer a penalty, you may find that more than one of your sites is affected ("tarred with the same brush"), but the cost of using different blocks is generally high and the risk-reduction benefits are relatively low.

The multiple-domain hosting option is very attractive, however. You may decide to host a blog alongside your business site (a great idea that I will cover later, page 167). You may decide to branch out into different business niches (an idea I covered in the business proposition section earlier, page 27). Either way, if you have to pay separately to host these, your costs will quickly mount up, as will the complexity of administering your different sites.

One final technical point on the flexibility of your hosting provider. Ask them a few questions about their support for regular server-side SEO activities. For example, do they allow you to edit your .htaccess file? Do they support both 301 redirects and mod_rewrite URL modification? I will cover both later in more detail, but suffice to say, these should be pretty key factors in your decision at this stage.

Resellers

It may have come to your attention that most hosting providers resell their hosting space through their (primary) customers. Reseller hosting is similar to what happens with office properties when a lessee sublets a property to someone else. The ultimate owner may not be the person you are letting from.

However, did you know that sometimes resellers also sell to other resellers? Or that those re-resellers sometimes sell on to re-re-resellers? If you purchase web space at a suspiciously low monthly cost, you may want to check who you are actually buying from. It could be someone operating from the bedroom of their house!

My advice is where possible to deal directly with the actual owner of the servers your site will sit on. The longer the reseller chain, the more likely it is that any one company in the chain could go bust. The first you will know about this is when your site goes down and you can't find out whom to retrieve your data from. Getting decent support for service issues can also be more challenging with deeply nested reseller arrangements. How many phone calls do you want to make before you find someone who can actually help you?

While none of these reseller issues is SEO related, they are all nonetheless an important part of your planning. Doing some detailed research up front – and not simply shopping on lowest price – is a prerequisite.

Key points on hosting

Do not underestimate the importance of choosing the right web-hosting provider. This is not an area where you should make cuts in your budget. If your SEO campaign is not based on the firm foundations of a strong technical platform, Googlebot and its friends will shun your site.

- ✧ Choose a fast host with modern servers and high-bandwidth connections.
- ✧ Choose a reliable host that demonstrably minimizes downtime.
- ✧ Use Linux for hosting unless other (functional) needs dictate otherwise.

✧ Choose a host with servers in the country where most of your customers live.

✧ Do consider multiple-domain hosting packages.

✧ Look for flexibility and decent support arrangements.

✧ Avoid deeply nested reseller arrangements.

Choosing your domain name

Once you have the right hosting environment, it is time to consider your domain name. Since the very earliest days of the mass-market internet, people have spent anything from a dollar to $14 million (on sex.com) to acquire keyword-rich domain names.

It's time to dust off that list of keywords. Remember the keyword-deployment principles of prominence, proximity, and density? Well, here's a newsflash: One of the most effective places to deploy your keywords is in the first full text block that Google sees, the full URL of each and every page on your site. The full URL comprises the domain name, the directory structure, and the filename. For example:

http://www.yourdomain.com/product-categoryA/product1.html

As prominence remains the most important of the three deployment principles, it is the domain name itself that you must consider first, as it appears closest to the front of this text block. We will cover the directory structure and filename in a later section (page 86).

You may have read on SEO forums that keyword-rich domain names are a waste of time, that users see them as spammy, and that brand presence is more important. As usual, there is some truth in all these arguments, but recognize that if you choose to follow this advice, you are opting not to use one of the most powerful SEO tools at your disposal.

Try typing "search" into Google and you might expect to see Google first in the results (not least because Google owns the search engine you are using). However, at time of writing, search.live.com ranks highest. Google does not even feature in the top 10! This is despite the fact that search.live.com does not have a PageRank to compare with Google itself and has a tiny market share when compared to what are considered to be the top two (Google and Yahoo!). Note how each appearance of the word "search" is highlighted by Google in bold in the results pages (including the domain names). I rest my case: Domain names do matter.

I know what you're thinking: All the good keyword-rich domain names have gone by now. You might be surprised (as you will soon see with Brad). You might also be concerned that Google views keyword-loaded domain names as spam. Finally, you might prefer to use your business name as your URL. I will deal with all three of these concerns (in reverse order) below.

First, let's look at the business name versus keyword-rich domain name decision. I appreciate that typing "search" alone into Google is hardly a scientific test. However, why not try any number of keyword searches and have a good look at the top 20 results for each? You can't help but notice the number of sites that contain your keywords in their domain name (or at the very least their full URL).

The bottom line is that after you – and your competitors – have used every other piece of optimization available, your domain name selection is perhaps the only area where you can really differentiate your-self. This is precisely because so many of your competitors are unwilling (or unable) to change to a keyword-rich domain. As such, it may be your only realistic chance in this ever more mature market to achieve a top 10 ranking for some of your key search terms.

Secondly, you may be concerned that a keyword-rich domain name looks cheap or unprofessional. This is indeed a more valid concern. However, in my experience, it is the page title and description that entice people to click on a search result, rather than the domain name. Also, once they have recognized a keyword-rich domain name, they are more likely to remember it. Even (initially) offline businesses have used this strategy; after all, Toys "R" Us has quite a ring to it, doesn't it? Or think about Phones 4U in the UK.

I'm not going to go overboard with this, however. Some customers will be turned off by such a domain name. If you really cannot bear to use a keyword-rich domain for your main business site (and I would fully understand this), you could still consider acquiring one for use as your business blog. More on this later in the section on Web 2.0 (page 167).

Is there is a keyword-loading spam filter for domains? The general consensus (to which I subscribe, for once) is that Google tolerates a maximum of three keywords in a domain name but does not like more than three. While I cannot prove this, I can certainly vouch for a large number of three-word domains that perform well on the search engines. Current good examples of this (on Google.co.uk) include www.advancedmp3players.co.uk (#1 for "mp3 players") and www.diyswimmingpools.co.uk (#1 for "swimming pools"). Try a few more searches on common consumer items and you'll see what I mean.

But how do you find a suitable, keyword-rich domain name? Haven't all the good domain names already gone?

FORUM TOOLS On the forum (www.seo-expert-services.co.uk) I list a number of tools you can use to find suitable domains. One is at Webconfs.com (see www.webconfs.com/keyword-rich-domain-suggestions.php), which suggests two-word combinations from a one-word search, three-word combos from a two-word search, and so on. The tool even corrects your spelling errors.

The best domain name lookup tools go beyond your immediate enquiry and search for known popular keyphrase variants of your chosen phrase. As an example, try entering "wedding invitation." Notice how the tool suggests domains like "free-wedding-invitation" and "unique-wedding-invitation" and gives search popularity numbers for both. If you pay a visit and enter, in turn, the best KOI one-word and two-word keyphrases from the A list on your spreadsheet, I am prepared to bet that at least one suitable domain name will be available to you. If you don't believe me, give it a try!

Did you notice all the hyphens in the list of suggestions? Is it better to have underscores, hyphens, or nothing between the words in your domain name? You absolutely should *not* use underscores. Matt Cutts has confirmed on his blog that Google does not recognize underscores as equivalent to spaces between words. My personal preference is for hyphens, for the following reasons:

✧ While Google can distinguish and separate words without spaces from each other pretty well, some other search engines are not so clever.

✧ Hyphens separate out the words more clearly and are thus easier on the eye for the human reader.

✧ By using hyphens in your domain name, you can readily repeat these in your directory structure and file names later (creating a simple but effective consistency throughout your site).

Brad makes a visit to a keyword-rich domain tool and finds to his surprise that many frequently searched options that are relevant to his business are still available, including:

✧ printing-service.biz (62,297 daily searches)
✧ online-business-printing.com (115 daily searches)

Brad snaps them up, in preference to the four-word combinations online-business-card-printing.com and business-card-printing-service.com (which are also available). However, following emotional discussions with his family, he decides not to use either of these for the main business site (currently chambersprint.com), but instead sets the domains aside for future use as complementary business blog sites.

Challenging age deflation

I am still assuming at this point that you are setting up a new site from scratch. At this point you may feel pretty happy. After all, you have an advantage over those who have a site already: You can pick the right host and the right domain name. However, as you will see in the off-page section ("landing the links", page 131), Google operates an age-deflation factor in ranking websites, assuming that relatively young sites are less reliable for searches. This is a particular issue for new sites, as both the domain and all inbound links (other sites linking to yours) are affected by this deflation. The ageing delay was designed to prevent unscrupulous spammers from setting up 1,000 spam sites for Viagra in a single week, then deleting them when detected and setting them up again somewhere else.

However, while you may wait anything from 6–12 months or more to start ranking well, you can still use this time wisely to build inbound links (see page 134) and to fine-tune your copywriting skills. At this point you may be rather depressed, but, at the risk of pointing out the obvious, 12 months really isn't all that long in business terms. The Google ageing-delay filter has really served to make the online world much like the offline. It takes time for any business to become known and promoted. Fly-by-night Viagra sites are now just that and the serious businesspeople among us have nothing to fear other than a short delay.

Buying an existing domain

Assuming you are impatient to progress (as new webmasters often are) and cannot bear to wait the 6–12 months required for a new domain to rank well, you might want to look at acquiring a privately held or expired domain name. The sites overleaf (all offering similar services) may be a good place to start. Note that many domains are listed with more than one of these sites.

Domain broker	Directory URL	PageRank
Name Jet	www.namejet.com	Acquires expired or soon-to-be-deleted domains direct
Sedo	www.sedo.com	Domain broker services and auctions
Snap Names	www.snapnames.com	Sells expired and privately owned domains
Deleted Domains	www.deleteddomains.com	Searches for and buys deleted or forfeited domains
Pool.com	www.pool.com	Backorders and open auctions of expired and private domains

Bear in mind that Google tries to simulate the real world as far as possible. If one business acquires or merges with another, you would expect the PageRank (see page 129) and incoming links of the two businesses to carry across to the new entity. This is indeed what happens, so if you buy an active domain (in a private auction) and use proper redirects (see page 80) you have nothing to fear.

However, if you buy a defunct domain "off the shelf," there is really no reason you should acquire any of the goodwill that the now deceased business used to enjoy. Google actively discourages the practice of buying up old domains simply to escape the age delay, and many buyers of deleted domains find the PageRank they thought they were getting wiped out soon after their purchase.

I would suggest that if you are interested in a domain that is about to expire, you contact the actual domain name holder and seek to acquire the domain privately by mutual agreement, prior to its expiry. The whole process from domain expiry date to actual domain deletion from the ICANN (Internet Corporation for Assigned Names and Numbers, which manages domain names) database actually takes up to 75 days, so there should be plenty of time to agree a deal.

However, should you find yourself cutting it close, there is a risk that Google might incorrectly treat your change of ownership as a deleted domain firesale. My advice, in such a situation, is to keep as many of the Whois details the same for at least six months after your acquisition of the domain (using the same domain name registrar and web-hosting provider as the previous owner). Make the change look as much like a going-concern transfer as possible to mitigate the risk.

2.3 Managing an existing site

So what if you have an existing site? You may be breathing a sigh of relief that the Google age-deflation factor is not an issue for you (particularly if you have been up and running for more than a year). However, you may also be worried about your hosting provider or missing out on a keyword-rich domain. In this section I consider how you can address both of these issues.

Moving to a new hosting provider

If you have a simple HTML-based site, moving hosting providers is not a particularly difficult process, whether you are doing it yourself or asking your web-design firm to do it for you. You simply:

- ✧ Set up a new hosting account.
- ✧ Move all your server files onto a PC.
- ✧ Upload your server files and directory structure to the new host.
- ✧ Arrange for your domain name to be repointed at the new site.

There are two ways to achieve the repointing:

✧ Keep your existing hosting provider as your domain name registrar but ask it to update its domain name server (DNS) records to point at the DNS of your new provider.

✧ Begin the process of having your registrar changed to your new hosting provider (who will then handle everything for you).

The latter process takes longer overall (perhaps a few weeks). Either way, the final DNS change takes up to 48 hours to replicate across the whole internet. More help on this can be found via the forum (www.seo-expert-services.co.uk).

Moving to a new domain

Let's imagine for a moment that British Airways has opened up a new office in Greenland (to take advantage of global climate change). Let's further imagine that it wants to start up www.ba.gl and move some Greenland content from its main site to the new one. There is no fair reason a search engine should prevent the old pages from ranking the same, simply because they are now on a new domain. Fortunately, Google agrees and has issued guidelines to webmasters about how to place so-called 301 redirects on their sites when moving content to a new domain.

A 301 redirect tells search engines (and human browsers) that content has permanently moved from one location to another, and automatically redirects the user to the new page. Suffice to say, a 301 redirect (properly executed) will normally allow the target page on the new domain to escape the worst effects of age deflation.

If you are using a web-design firm to manage your website, it should be able to quote you a reasonable cost for undertaking such redirects. For those of you doing it yourself, I will now take you through the (unavoidably detailed) instructions on how to do this properly.

Undertaking 301 redirects

Before you begin, you need to ensure that your web-hosting provider will actually support the 301 redirection method you plan to use. While most will, several smaller providers may not. Go to the provider's FAQ or support page and find out whether the servers used support the .htaccess protocol and allow you to edit the file. If the provider does not support the standard, your only alternative is to move to a provider that does first, then undertake your redirection.

Again, before you start, note that the method used varies depending on whether you are on a UNIX or a Windows server (you may need to check with your hosting provider if you are unsure). I will describe examples of both methods, but be aware that there are other ways of doing this and if in doubt consult an expert.

301 redirects on a Unix server

Start by copying (or republishing) your entire site from the old server to the new. Next, check the root directory of the web server on your old server for a file called .htaccess; it will most probably not be there unless you or your webmaster created it previously. If one doesn't already exist, create it using any plain-text editor (like Windows NotePad), then name the file .htaccess (note no file extension of .txt or anything else, just a period followed by htaccess). If your site's root domain already contains an .htaccess file, you can open it using a text editor, then simply scroll to the end of whatever code is already there and append your 301 redirect code to the bottom of the file, starting on a new line. What you then type depends on what you want to achieve:

To redirect a whole site:
 ✧ redirect 301 / http://www.newdomain.com/

To redirect the contents of a directory (e.g., /olddir) and all its subdirectories:
 ✧ redirect 301 /olddir http://www.newdomain.com/newdir/

To redirect (in this example two) different single pages:
 ✧ redirect 301 /olddir/page1.html http://www.newdomain.com/ newdir/contact-us.html
 ✧ redirect 301 /olddir/page2.html http://www.newdomain.com/ newdir/testimonials.html

Note that the first part of the redirect is the current location and the second part is the new destination. In the single pages example, the webmaster has taken advantage of the redirect as an opportunity to rename her pages (from the cryptic page1.html to contact-us.html and from page2.html to testimonials.html).

Once you have saved the .htaccess file, you need to upload it to your server. Note that the right way to do this is:

 ✧ Remove any .txt file extension that your text editor may have added to the file name.
 ✧ Do the FTP transfer in ASCII rather than binary mode.
 ✧ Ensure that the file has the right Unix permissions.

The latter point requires a bit more explanation, but you would be very unlucky to have to change the permissions (so don't fret). Once you have completed the first two steps above, simply test the 301 redirect by trying to visit the old page in your browser. It should redirect you to the new location. If, however, you get a 403 (Forbidden Message) error, then you have a permissions problem and need to undertake the third step above. Use your FTP command line interface to change the Unix permissions on the .htaccess file to 644 (-rw-r–r–). The command to do this is chmod 644 .htaccess.

This may all seem very technical but, believe me, it is less scary than it sounds. As a purchaser of this book, you have free access to my SEO forum (www.seo-expert-services.co.uk). On the forum you can get help from me and fellow webmasters to get you over any hurdles.

301 redirects on a Windows server

On a Windows server you have to do all your redirection at page level. This can be a time-consuming exercise. The way you do it will also depend on whether you have coded your pages in ASP or ASP.NET. Here is what you need to do:

ASP pages
Place the following code at the very top of your web page code (i.e. above your <html> tag or <!DOCTYPE>, if you have one):
```
<%@ Language=VBScript %>
<%
response.status="301 moved permanently"
Response.AddHeader "Location", "http://www.newdomain.com/
new-file-directory/new-filename.html"
%>
```

ASP.NET pages
Again, place the code at the very top of your web page:
```
<script runat="server">
private void Page_Load(object sender, System.EventArgs e)
```

```
{
response.status = "301 moved permanently";
Response.AddHeader("Location,"  http://www.newdomain.com/
new-file-directory/new-filename.html");
}
</script>
```

The URL after "Location" should be the exact location to which
you want the page to redirect.

Losing backlinks pointing to your old domain

Your head is probably spinning now (apologies for that), but I'm afraid
there's yet one more challenge for the migrating webmaster to consider,
if a new, keyword-rich domain is indeed your goal. This challenge dwarfs
even that of 301 redirects: losing backlinks pointing to your site.

Backlinks are links to your site from other sites on the web. You will
find out more about them later, in the off-page optimization section
(page 132). However for now, all you need to know is that this is the
single most important aspect of your SEO campaign.

I will keep this really simple. If you already have more than 200
well-established backlinks to your old site and you are planning an entire
site migration, I would consider carefully whether the new domain is
really worth it. How do you find out how many backlinks you have? For
a start, Google and Alexa (which shows Google data) are not reliable
sources. Google only shows a sample of the backlinks that any site has.
For a more complete picture, my preferred source is Yahoo! Site
Explorer.

To find out your number of backlinks on Yahoo!, go to the search
box and enter the command link:http://www.yourdomain.com before
hitting enter. Following your redirection to Yahoo! Site Explorer, on the

results page select the option "Except from this domain" under "Show inlinks" to filter out internal site links.

While, as I have said, a 301 redirect will pass the PageRank of the old page to the new (and thus preserve the value of the inbound links at that time) I have observed that the value of this appears to diminish over time. As such, I recommend to all my clients that if they have inbound links to old URLs, they contact each linking site and directory owner in turn, and ask them to change their link to the new location. If you do not do this (or they do not comply), then the PageRank of your pages will decline over time, even with the 301 redirection correctly in place. As a fair percentage of site owners will not bother, this is why I do not recommend an unavoidable migration to anyone who already has lots of backlinks in place.

Where you are creating new content (which by definition has no backlinks yet) or migrating a site with only a limited number of back-links, my advice is different: You should absolutely migrate your domain or directory to a more search-engine-friendly domain name and struc-ture now, while your number of backlinks is low. Otherwise, it will be much more painful later.

If you decide to move to a new domain name, remember:

✧ Register it as soon as you have made the decision.
✧ Start writing the content for it in a part of your existing site.
✧ Move the content from the old site to the new about three to four months after you create the new domain.
✧ 301 redirect search engine spiders from the old site to the new.

If you are lucky, Google will pick this up quickly as a permanent move and the new domain will flip into the main index right away.

2.4 Site structure and navigation

Whether you have an existing site or a new one, you need to pay close attention to the <u>structure</u> of your site to court the Google crawl. You will remember that the entire URL of each page is the first (and arguably the most important) text block that Googlebot encounters on your page. We have dealt with the most prominent part of that URL, the domain name. It is now time to move on through the URL to the directory structure and the filenames you use.

Optimizing your directory structure

After your domain name, the next most prominent opportunity for keyword deployment is the <u>directory name</u>. This brings us into the important area of site structure and navigation. You will remember from the "how Google finds" section (page 55) how Google crawls down through your site spreading PageRank like pixie dust across your pages. You might also remember the analogy of good sites being like a symmetrical tree (with the directories being the branches and the pages being the leaves).

My recommendations (for the non-secure, http: section of your site) are as follows:

⬧ Limit your site <u>depth</u> to no more than four levels if at all possible (i.e., so that any given page is no more than three clicks down the navigation from the homepage). If you can, shoot for just three levels.

⬧ Limit your site <u>span</u> to no more than eight, where span is the maximum number of pages that sit under another page in the navigation.

⬧ This gives an overall maximum number of pages of $1+(8^3) = 513$, which should be more than enough for all but the most content-rich of sites.

⬦ If you do have a bigger site, jump onto my forum for some
   advice and I will be happy to help (but in general, simply tick up
   the numbers, e.g., to five levels and a span of ten).

For a four-level site structure (compliant with my rules on symmetry), I
use the following terminology to describe the different levels (based on
the excellent Joomla! content-management system):

⬦ Homepage – the top-most page on your site.
⬦ Section pages – the next level down (each with their own
   directory).
⬦ Category pages – the next level down (again with their own
   directory).
⬦ Content pages – the next level down from that.

In our maximum expansion site, 1+8+64=73 of the pages would be
devoted to homepage, section, and category pages, which essentially
introduce the next levels down. This leaves 513–73=440 available for
actual content pages. Perhaps the best way to illustrate this approach is
to use poor old Brad once again as an example.

Brad opts for a symmetrical site structure. The following URLs
demonstrate how this works for his business card product line:

Homepage:
http://www.chambersprint.com/index.html

Section page:
http://www.chambersprint.com/business-printing/business-
printing.html

Category page:
http://www.chambersprint.com/business-printing/business-cards/

business-card-printing.html

<u>Content pages:</u>
http://www.chambersprint.com/business-printing/business-cards/
luxury-business-cards.html
http://www.chambersprint.com/business-printing/business-
cards/cheap-business-cards.html
etc.

As you can see, the nature of Brad's business has led him to use
sections to serve different customer segments, categories to group
different product types, and content pages to deal with product
lines. You may find that the same works for you.

You will note that I generally recommend two-word keyphrases for both
sections and categories, but three-word keyphrases for content page filenames, all hyphenated. This gives you plenty of scope to deploy the
phrases that pay – with appropriate proximity – in this all-important text
block. The overall length of the URL also provides suitable, natural
opportunities for improved keyword density.

The directory structure is logical and helps orientate the human
reader to where they are in the site. The fact that this works well for
search engines also is merely a happy coincidence.

For avoidance of confusion, I do not think of the following types of
pages as being part of my 1+(8^3) rule:

✧ Website terms of use, delivery terms, etc. (as the footer of all
  pages).
✧ Privacy policy, Contact us, etc. (also for the footer of all pages).
✧ Secure server pages for online ordering (Google will not crawl
  these).
✧ Pages you need to log in to access (Google won't crawl either).
✧ Sitemap (linked from homepage).

Optimizing file names and extensions

You will have noted from the case study examples above that the <u>file names</u> for the pages themselves are also part of the optimization campaign (with a three-word, hyphenated pattern the recommendation). You might also have noticed that all the pages end in .html. Personally, I would always opt for static .html file extensions where possible. Although Google's new, Mozilla-based crawler is better at handling dynamic extensions (dynamic web pages change each time they are viewed, for example to show the current time or a different picture), more complex URLs that include "?" or "%" in the query string may still consign your pages to the dreaded supplemental index (which I cover in the next section, page 94).

Many content-management and ecommerce solutions, however, do generate dynamic file names. I am a fan and a user of many of these, including my personal favourite, Joomla! The question remains: How do you handle dynamic URLs? Fortunately, there is an answer: mod_rewrite. Again, this is somewhat technical, so feel free to skip this section.

Using mod_rewrite

The <u>mod_rewrite</u> standard is used to rewrite URLs at the server level (standing between the request from a browser for that page and how the server renders that page). This means that someone requesting the static page www.yourdomain.com/widgets/blue.html may actually be served the dynamic page www.yourdomain.com/widgets.php?color=blue by the server, unaware of the technical wizardry behind the scenes.

To use mod_rewrite, you need a hosting provider that supports its use. If you are using the Apache web server program there is a way to check, either by looking at the httpd.conf file or by running a php query on your php.info file. However, rather than describe this in depth here, can I suggest you simply contact your web-hosting support team and ask them the question? For the rest of this section, I will assume that they answered yes. If they answered no, perhaps it is time to look at another host.

Remember our evaluation of 301 redirects and our friend the .htaccess file? We return to this file to implement mod_rewrite. In the simple example below, the addition of this code rewrites any browser request for the page http://www.yourdomain.com/apple.html to http://www.your domain.com/orange.html:

RewriteEngine on
RewriteRule ^apple.html$ orange.html

The content of orange.html will be displayed to the user, but the URL that appears in the browser window will be apple.html. While this may all sound very simple, creating the right mod_rewrite instructions for a complex set of dynamic URLs is not for the faint-hearted, as you need to use complex conditional operators. The developer of any commercial software that writes dynamic URLs should have sufficient knowledgebase support for mod_rewrite (at least on Apache servers). Others have whole back-end modules that you can plug in and then use yourself without fear. Hassle the developer, read their FAQs, and insist on some help. Persevere until you get it right, but if you can't, get onto my support forum for some assistance.

You may have heard that you can't use mod_rewrite on Windows servers. This is not actually true, you can. However, implementing mod_rewrite in Windows (e.g., to rewrite .aspx files) is much more complicated than in Apache. You may well find you need professional help from a developer and possibly a trip to www.getafreelancer.com. However, it is worth it, so don't give up.

Phase 2
The SEO campaign

Step 3: Priming your pages

In courting the crawl you learnt how to lay the appropriate site-wide foundations for your site, including domain name, hosting provider, and site structure. It is now time to move to optimization of the individual web pages themselves (plus the images, documents, videos, and other assets that comprise your website asset files).

I call this process <u>priming your pages</u> and it is the part of SEO that people most readily understand and enjoy. Why do I call it priming? I'm borrowing the term from painting and decorating. Priming your wall surface before you paint it is vital if you are to achieve the right overall result at the end. On-page SEO is like priming and off-page SEO (the section on "landing the links", page 128) is like painting. Neither will be effective without the other.

In courting the crawl we first explored how Google finds sites. Similarly, before we get into on-page SEO, we should look at how Google stores information.

3.1 How Google stores information

If a search engine had to sequentially scan every word in (say) 500,000 documents to find all mentions of the word(s) you are searching for, the process could take hours. The purpose of an <u>index</u>, therefore, is to optimize the speed and performance of a search query by breaking down documents into the keywords they contain.

This whole process is not too dissimilar to the old card indexes you might remember in public libraries. To read through every book in the library looking for the words "gulf war" might take you a lifetime. Even scanning the titles might take you several hours. However, flicking through a card index took a matter of minutes and normally helped you to locate the resources you needed.

While the use of an index speeds up information retrieval, the trade-offs are the massive amount of additional storage required to hold the index and the considerable time and effort needed to keep that index up to date. Google has somewhere between 500,000 and 1,000,000 servers, spread out over more than 70 data centers and several thousand acres of land. Its computing requirements continue to expand rapidly!

How Google builds its index

Once Googlebot has crawled your site, it gives a unique ID to each page it has found and passes these to an indexing program. This lists every document that contains a certain word. For example, the word "gulf" might exist in documents 4, 9, 22, 57, and 91, while the word "war" might be found in documents 3, 9, 15, 22, 59, and 77. If someone were to search with the query "gulf war," only documents 9 and 22 would contain both words.

Google stop words

The Google Search box ignores certain common words, such as "where" and "how," as well as certain single digits and letters. In its official FAQ Google says, "these terms rarely help narrow a search and can slow search results." Of course, the main reason such words are not indexed is because doing so would massively increase the Google index (at great computing cost and with limited user benefit).

These stop words include (but are not limited to) i, a, about, an, and, are, as, at, be, by, for, from, how, in, is, it, of, on, or, that, the, this, to, was, what, when, where, who, will, with.

However, Google is quite intelligent at recognizing when a stop word is being used in a way that is uncommon. So, for example, a search for "the good, the bad and the ugly" will be read by Google as "good bad ugly." However, a search for "the who" will not be ignored but will be processed as it is, returning results for the well-known rock band.

How Google stores the index

Google makes this process quicker by using hundreds of computers to store its index. When a query is processed, the task of identifying the pages containing the query words is divided among many machines, speeding up the task immensely. To return to our library analogy, if one person had to search a 70-page index in a book to find one phrase that did not occur in the main alphabetical sequence, it might take up to a minute to locate the text. However, if 70 people each had a page of the index and were working as a team, this task would take a few seconds at most.

How Google interrogates the index

The list of documents that contain a word is called a <u>posting list</u>, and looking for documents with more than one word is called "intersecting a posting list." Our intersected list in the gulf war example above contains documents 9 and 22.

Google's search engine essentially performs two tasks:

- ✧ Finding the set of pages (from the index) that contain the user's query somewhere.
- ✧ Ranking the matching pages in order of importance and relevance.

I cover the latter in greater depth in the section on "landing the links" (page 128).

The supplemental index

For several years now Google has maintained two separate indexes, referred to as the main index and the supplemental index. The number of pages appearing in the supplemental index increased substantially in early 2006. The understanding people have of the supplemental index is still evolving, informed partly by limited explanations of how it works from Google, both official and unofficial. However, there are certain features that have become clear and that you need to be aware of:

✧ Pages that trigger spam filters are more likely to be removed from the index altogether than to be placed in the supplemental index; the supplemental index is not a form of penalty that can be lifted through requests to be reincluded.

✧ Pages in the supplemental index are less likely to be returned to users undertaking a search and less likely to be ranked well in the search results served to users.

✧ Pages are very likely to end up in the supplemental index if they closely match pages elsewhere on your site (so-called duplicate content).

✧ Pages may end up in the supplemental index if they closely match pages on other sites that are cited more often than yours (i.e., where you appear to have syndicated – or even plagiarized – content).

✧ Pages from very large sites may end up in the supplemental index if insufficient PageRank has been passed to the page (more on this later, page 129).

✧ Pages that are hard to crawl (e.g., because they use too many parameters in a URL or are larger than 101k) may end up in the supplemental index.

✧ According to Google's unofficial spokesperson Matt Cutts, the pages held in the supplemental index are parsed differently and held in the form of a "compressed summary," meaning that "not every single word in every single phrase relationship" has been fully indexed.

Scary, eh? Despite Google's attempts to placate webmasters – and to insist that ending up in the supplemental index is no tragedy – for some website owners the changes have been calamitous, with many hundreds of their pages disappearing into relative obscurity. Perhaps this is why Google has recently taken steps to hide which pages are in the supplemental index, by removing the supplemental marker from search engine results pages.

You might wonder why Google bothers with a supplemental index at all if it is so controversial. There are two simple reasons: quality and cost effectiveness. Five years ago, the search engine market was all about who had the biggest index (the so-called size wars). Today, with the number of web pages stretching into the billions, the challenge is much more about quality than quantity. Less is, in fact, more. Google has recognized this and is trying to find ways to present an ever leaner and better-quality set of results.

Not indexing every single word and phrase relationship in the supplemental index also saves Google money over the long term, as it does not need to purchase as many servers and data centers. It can also manage and limit its carbon footprint and help the environment. The latter goes down well with stakeholders.

There are, in practice, two main SEO steps you should take to counter the effects of the supplemental index. I cover these in greater depth later on, but for now a simple summary should suffice:

✧ Ensure that the navigation of your site is even. If the structure of your site is like a tree, with the directories being the branches and the pages the leaves, your tree should look symmetrical, rather than lopsided, if you want the life-giving sap of PageRank to pass evenly down through to each and every page.

✧ Try to ensure that at least 10–15% of all the inbound links to your site are "deep links" to important internal content or category pages.

✧ Test pages on your site that might be too similar to one another using tools like the Similar Page Checker at www.webconfs.com/similar-page-checker.php. If the page pairs fail the test (or you have a strong suspicion they may already be in the supplemental index), consider rewriting them from scratch and giving them different URLs (without using 301 redirects). This should get you a fresh start.

✧ Make sure that the URLs do not contain too many parameters and that the size of each page is less than 100k.

To find out which of your pages are in the supplemental index, the most reliable technique is to compare your total pages indexed to the total pages in the main index (which can still be identified):

✧ To get total pages indexed, type into Google:
  site:www.yourdomain.com
✧ To get pages in the main index, type into Google:
  site:www.yourdomain.com -inallurl:www.yourdomain.com
✧ Pages in supplemental index = Total pages indexed – Pages in the main index.

By printing off and comparing the two lists, you can work out which pages on your site are in the supplemental index. If you can't find a single one, well done! If you find loads, don't panic. Simply follow the instructions above and persevere. If you really struggle to shake off the supplementals, give me a shout on the forum and I will see what I can do to help.

3.2 On-page optimization

You remember my insistence on having the right (keyword) ingredients before attempting to cook your meal? Or my assertion that 20% of your time should be spent on preparing those ingredients? Having learnt about phrases that pay, you will understand why. Optimization effort spent on a poor set of keywords is a fruitless exercise. In this section, you are (finally) ready to get cooking with your keywords.

On-page SEO means all the techniques that you can use on your own site; as distinct from off-page SEO, which is all the techniques you can get other site owners to use that will help your site to rank well. These techniques apply to all the content of your web servers, including your pages and other assets (such as Word documents, PDF files, videos, and more).

The on-page elements include page titles, page metadata, headings, body text, internal links, off-page links, and image alt tags, as well as a host of other assets. I will walk through each item in turn, in the order in which they generally appear in a well-formed HTML page. For each item, I will show you what to do for best effect and consider the overall importance of the item in the mix. I cover asset optimization in a separate section (page 115).

Page title

The very first variable element on your page is the <title> tag, which appears in the <head> section. The title of your web page is probably the most important of all the on-page elements to get right for four reasons:

- ✧ Algorithmic weighting. The title is the most important single summary of what a page is all about and therefore carries the highest on-page weighting in the Google algorithm.
- ✧ Results formatting. When Google serves up search engine results pages (SERPs) for a user query, it uses the page title as the link for each result. As such, it is the most important "call to action" for users, who might then click on the result and enter your page. Does your title make them want to click?
- ✧ Browser usability. Browsers display the title tag in the top bar of the browser window and, in more recent browser versions, for tabbed navigation between different web pages in the same window. Thus, the title is also an important navigation usability aid for browser users.

✧ <u>Directory submission</u>. Some directory and librarian services insist on using the page title for listing any links or deep links to your site. They also prefer titles that include, at the front, the name of your site or business. This applies to both human-edited and some more automated directory services.

Given these four different roles, optimizing your title tag is a multi-faceted problem. For a good SEO title, you want to deploy your phrases that pay in appropriate prominence, proximity, and density. For a good call to action, you want a short phrase that catches the eye and invites readers to do something that benefits both them and you (typically in a verb–noun construct like "subscribe to my free report"). For a browser window description, you want something that clearly distinguishes your page from others that the user might have open at the same time and orients them to where they are in your site. For a directory listing, you want something that looks well organized and includes (in every case) the name of the site.

Before I recommend the appropriate balance between these factors, it is necessary to consider <u>title length</u>. Theoretically, there is no limit to how long a title tag can be. However in practice, both search engines and browsers truncate long titles to make their display consistent. W3C (World Wide Web Consortium) guidelines state that the length of the title tag should, ideally, be 64 characters (including spaces) or less. Google truncates at 66 characters or the last complete full word, whichever is the smaller. Yahoo! simply truncates at exactly 120 characters, even if this means that the displayed title ends partway through a word. At the other extreme, anything over 75 characters is truncated in the top bar title display of some browsers (although some versions may support up to 95).

So, here are my recommendations for constructing your title tag. These are principles rather than hard rules. Achieving all of them at the same time will generally be impossible, so juggle them to get the best overall result for you.

✧ Every page must have a title tag and each page's title tag should be different. There should, nonetheless, be consistency across the pages in how the title tags have been constructed.

✧ The length of each title tag should generally not exceed 85 characters (including spaces) and should never exceed 120 characters.

✧ The title should be written in such a way that it gracefully truncates at both 66 characters exactly and 75 characters exactly (including spaces). By gracefully, I mean complete words in a phrase that scans well and uses proper grammar.

✧ The title tag should ideally begin with the name of your business or site and, where possible, should be written in the form of a "breadcrumb trail" that leads users down through the levels of your site (see page 106).

✧ Where possible, the title tag should incorporate a short call to action (in a verb–noun construct), or at the very least a provocative statement that encourages the user to click on the link.

✧ The keywords used in the title tag should all be repeated in the URL, the meta-keyword tag, heading tags, and page body text. Synonyms of keywords in the title tag should also appear in the page body text.

If this sounds challenging, it is! Writing a good title tag is second only to writing good pay-per-click ad text in terms of a copywriting challenge. Let's consider some examples, using Brad's business as our case study.

> Brad works hard on the copywriting of his page title for the luxury business cards product line. He begins with the URL of the page, which you will remember is http://www.chambersprint.com/ business-printing/business-cards/luxury-business-cards.html.
>
> His first effort combines the business name, the breadcrumb trail, and a verb–noun call to action in one long construct:

Chambers Business Printing > Business Printing > Business Cards > Luxury Business Cards – Design and Order Luxury Business Cards Online

However, this first stab at the title is too long at 135 characters (including spaces). Brad knows, from the advice in this book, that his title will be truncated in the following ways:

✧ Yahoo! SERPs will display Chambers Business Printing > Business Printing > Business Cards > Luxury Business Cards – Design and Order Luxury Busine
✧ Google SERPs will display Chambers Business Printing > Business Printing > Business Cards... [63 characters – truncated to last full word]
✧ A 75-character browser title bar would show Chambers Business Printing > Business Printing > Business Cards > Luxury Bu

After much editing and further ruthless copywriting, Brad gets down to:

Chambers > Business Printing > Order Luxury Business Cards Online

At 65 characters, the full title will now be displayed without truncation in Google, Yahoo!, and the browser title bar. The full name of the business is retained (and is proximate, i.e., near the keywords). The section structure of the URL is also there at least (even if he has had to lose the category). Most importantly, the phrase that pays for this particular money page ("luxury business cards") is included, proximate, and enjoys a reasonable density of $21/65 = 32\%$.

Brad continues in a similar vein with all his other pages. For section pages, he uses a longer construct that truncates well for Google but is visible in full on Yahoo!:

Chambers > Business Printing > Business Cards, Letterheads &
more: Compliment Slips, Leaflets, Flyers, Address Labels

This will appear in Google as:

Chambers > Business Printing > Business Cards, Letterheads & more

You might be wondering whether Brad could have done even better from
an SEO point of view. Well, you would be right. What you are trying to
do is *balance* all the four factors covered above, of which SEO is only
one. However, given the importance of the title tag, you should always
come down on the side of good SEO if there is a tradeoff to be made. If
Brad had been operating in a very competitive environment, my advice
would have been to opt for a very SEO-weighted construct, which maxi-
mizes prominence, proximity, and density (in that order). For example:

✧ Good: Order Luxury Business Cards Online
✧ Better: Luxury Business Cards – Order Business Cards Online
✧ Best: Luxury Business Cards – Order Luxury Business Cards
    Online

When you deploy your keywords, use the most effective site-wide
phrases in your homepage titles and use all of them in your section titles.
For category and content page titles, use your deep phrases.

Just one or two final points on title tags. First, you will notice the
use of capitalization throughout the examples (despite the fact that this
is poor grammar). There is a reason for this: Research has shown that
modest and appropriate use of capitalization makes your links stand
out, so people are more likely to click on them. Secondly, you will notice
the use of the ampersand (&) instead of the word "and." As I have
explained previously, words like "the", "an," and "and" are stop words
and are ignored by Google for most searches. As such, using them takes
up valuable space in your tag and should be avoided.

Meta description

The meta-description tag is placed between the <head> tags in your HTML page. Its purpose is to provide a brief synopsis of page content, which builds on the headline included in the title tags. The correct syntax is as follows:

<meta name="description" content="put your description in here." />

Most of the meta tags on a page carry very little SEO value. Search engines in general (and Google in particular) have paid less and less attention to them over time, because so many webmasters abuse them and their content is not actually displayed on the page. Arguably, several are even counterproductive, in that they make a page longer (and reduce both density and crawl efficiency) without adding any value. As such, you may see comments around the forums that the meta-description tag isn't that important. In some ways these comments are correct, if SEO is all you are focusing on. However, in fact the meta-description tag is very important for the following two (not strictly SEO) reasons:

✧ Snippet compilation. When Google creates search engine results pages, it may use the description tag in constructing the "call to action" snippet that appears below the results link. While this is more internet marketing than true SEO, I dedicate a whole section to the important area of SERPs and snippets (page 118).

✧ Directory submission. Some directory services pick up and use your page meta description as the description of your entry in their directory listings. This applies to both human-edited and some more automated directory services.

I will return to meta-description tags in the snippets section and show you there what Brad came up with for Chambers Print. However, for now, let's keep moving through the page.

Meta keyword

The meta-keyword tag (or tags) is also placed between the <head> tags in your HTML page and was intended solely for use by search engines. The idea is that the keyword tags provide information to the search engine about the contents of your page (as an aid to semantic indexing). The correct syntax is as follows:

<meta name="keywords" content="keyword1,keyword2,keywordn" />

I don't want to disappoint you, but I am afraid that the meta-keyword tag is almost useless for improving your position on Google. Over the last five years the tag has become so abused by spammers that Google now appears to ignore the tag altogether in determining the true meaning of a page.

However, I still consider meta-keyword tags to be worth pursuing, as there remains patchy (but genuine) evidence that Yahoo! and Ask.com results are still influenced by them (albeit typically only for pages that are very graphics intensive). This is due, in part, to the underlying origins of the search technology used by both engines (Inktomi and Teoma), which have always paid attention to keyword tags.

So on balance, I would not ignore keyword tags. After all, the exercise of working out what to put in them has value in itself, as it helps you to structure your thinking on how to deploy your A, B, and C keyword lists. As I said previously, SEO can be like throwing mud at a wall – while most of your meta-keyword mud will not stick on the wall, every little bit of effort can help. My recommendations are as follows:

✧ While spaces within keyword phrases are fine, you should separate each phrase with a comma and no space (e.g., "sharepoint 2007,moss 2007").

✧ Use lower case for all keywords and pluralize phrases where possible. Do not bother including capitalized or nonplural equivalents.

◈ Include all of your site-wide phrases at the front of the meta-keyword tag of the homepage. Exclude all deep phrases from the homepage tag.

◈ Use the most relevant site-wide phrases to begin your section and category page meta-keyword tags, and then also include the most relevant deep phrases.

◈ On content pages, confine yourself to deep phrases in the meta-keyword tags.

◈ Never use more than 50 words in the meta-keyword tag and ideally try to limit yourself to 35 words in each.

◈ Ensure that all of the keyphrases in your keyword tag appear at least once more somewhere in your on-page elements (i.e., title tag, description tag, headings, alt tags, and body text). If you can't achieve this, seriously consider removing the keyword from your tag.

Part of the reason I recommend that clients still prepare keyword tags is that the process of choosing them is useful in itself. Just as an essay is much improved by first writing an essay plan, so the copy on a web page can be much improved by first planning what words should be included.

> For his home page, Brad opts for the following 33 keywords, organized into 19 comma-separated units:
>
> chamber print,printers boise,printers idaho,business printers, business printing,business cards,letterhead printing,compliment slips,printed labels,address labels,custom labels,print design,leaflets,flyers, notepaper,business stationery,stationary,brochures,online printing
>
> Note the use of plurals, the lack of capitals and the inclusion of a common misspelling (stationary).

The C-shape

We now leave the <head> section behind and continue our journey through on-page elements by turning to the <body> section. Within your page body, there are five important elements from an SEO perspective: breadcrumb trail, heading tags, body text, image alt tags, and internal links/navigation bars.

For design purposes, the most important text blocks in your body generally appear nearest the top of the page, nearest the left of the page, and in the page footer. I refer to this as the C-shape. These areas are most important because of the way in which users are accustomed to reading a website, scanning through quickly rather than reading in full, and looking for key navigational areas along the way.

The general consensus is that search engine algorithms attempt to simulate, at least in part, this user behavior. For example, if a page is very long, some spiders grant extra weight to words at the left and bottom. Even if the page is short, extra weight is assigned to words at the top (a variant of the prominence principle we have seen already).

Breadcrumb trail

The breadcrumb trail is of immense value for usability and SEO value, so it is amazing how many sites neglect to use them. For your site, the breadcrumb trail is best served as:

Home Page » Section name » Category name » Page name – Page description

The symbol used to separate each element is a guillemet (»), which indicates the direction of travel (down through the levels of your site) and is rendered as » in HTML.

Note that each of the breadcrumb elements is linked to the relevant page in the navigation, so the section name link, for example, takes you to the section page. The best way to illustrate their use is to return to our case study.

> You will remember that Brad's first stab at a title for his luxury business cards content page was as follows:
>
> Chambers Business Printing – Business Printing – Business Cards – Luxury Business Cards – Design and Order Luxury Business Cards Online
>
> It may not surprise you to learn that this is absolutely perfect as a breadcrumb trail. Brad simply reproduces the trail above at the top of the page, using 8-point Verdana, color gray, and replacing the dash with a guillemet. Each of the elements is appropriately linked, to give:
>
> Chambers Business Printing » Business Printing » Business Cards » Luxury Business Cards – Design and Order Luxury Business Cards Online
>
> Note that the "luxury business cards" link actually links to the same page that this breadcrumb appears on.

You may wonder why breadcrumb trails have an SEO value. They deliver very well in three separate areas:

✧ Breadcrumb trails reinforce the navigational structure of the site so that PageRank is distributed evenly down through your pages.
✧ Breadcrumb trails are generally the first text that appears in the body of your page (which as we have seen attracts a prominence weighting) and thus afford you a legitimate reason to cram this vital real estate with your best keywords and keyphrases.

✧ Links to your pages that incorporate keyword-rich anchor text
(as we shall see later in the off-page optimization section, page
132) are always of value, even when those links come from other
pages in your own site. The breadcrumb trail gives you a legitimate opportunity to include more of these.

Heading tag

After the title tag, the heading tag is the next most important SEO on-
page element and I typically consider it to be twice as important in
weighting terms as regular body text. Nevertheless, surprisingly few websites (even major websites) make active use of it in their HTML. Just try
a random sample of 20 Fortune 500 companies and take a look through
their homepage source (view "Source" or "Page source" in your browser
menu). I am prepared to bet that barely 50% of your sample will have
made good and active use of heading tags.

Some webmasters try a heading tag once, only to grimace at how it
appears in their browser when it's published. "Ugh! All big and Times
New Roman" is the typical reaction. However, heading tags can be con-
trolled using style sheets in your web page software and made to look
very elegant. As such, there is no excuse for not using them.

Regular HTML supports up to six levels of heading tags:

✧ <h1>Your heading text</h1>
✧ <h2>First subheading</h2>
etc.

Each tag down carries slightly less SEO weighting than the one above.
For this reason, I find it pretty funny when I see a page with only <h2>
tags on it. Typically, I do not recommend using more than the <h1>
and <h2> tags on any given page. If you find yourself wanting to use
more, can I suggest instead that you break your content up into more
sections, categories, and pages? I also recommend using no more than

five to seven heading tags on any one page, to avoid diluting their value.

Heading tags are a great way to break up the content of your pages into more manageable chunks that are easier on the eye for the human reader. Even if they carried no SEO benefit at all, I would still use them.

Body text

For reasons of density, I recommend that clients include no more than 450–600 words in total on each page (and ideally near the lower end of that range). If you need more words, then look at using more sections, categories, and pages. Remember your human readers. Do they want to read through 5,000 words? Would they really take in each and every one or would they scan through, trying to pick out key pieces of information? In short, there are lots of good reasons to keep your body text concise.

Use **bold** – <bold> or <strong> – and *italics* – <em> or <i> – to pick out keywords on the page, but sparingly. This helps both search engines and human readers to identify your key text. But don't use the <u>underline</u> <u> tag anywhere on your page – it confuses users expecting to find a link!

I further recommend that body text is divided into neat paragraphs of no more than three or four sentences – using the paragraph tags <p></p> – and that your phrases that pay are positioned near the start of each paragraph where possible.

Obviously, I recommend that you sprinkle your two-, three-, and four-word keyword chains throughout the text, with reasonable frequency. Opinions differ on ideal keyword density. Much depends on how competitive your key words are and how many you are targeting seriously. For your top four (and site-wide) keywords, I would aim for a density of 20% for each individually in sector one on the homepage (where sector one is defined as title + headings + bold text + italicized text + alt text).

The general density for regular page text content (sector two) should be 2-4% for your page-specific (and most important) two-word keyphrases, 0.8-1.5% for your three-word chains, and 0.2-0.5% for related keywords (but plenty of them).

FORUM TOOLS To test the density of your overall page copy, you can make use of a <u>keyword density analyzer</u>. On the forum (www.seo-expert-services.co.uk) there are a series of links to the top-rated tools. For the purposes of this illustration I will use the iCrossing Keyword Page Analyser (currently at www.icrossing.co.uk/seotoolkit/seo-toolkit/page-analyser/).

Put the address of the page you wish to analyze into the query box and hit the button. The tool tells you first the number of words in sectors one and two, both including and excluding stop words. The total (excluding stop words) should be less than 600. Next, the tool shows you the density of the most common single, double, triple, and quadruple word phrases. Refer back to my guidelines above and check your keyphrases against these results. Go back and tweak your copywriting until you are happy with the results.

Never underestimate the importance of good SEO copywriting. It is the most challenging part of the work I do for clients (and the most time consuming). In your body text elements you have more freedom than in other text blocks. Try to use this freedom wisely.

Image alt tag

In all your copywriting activities you need to remember that web pages are designed for human beings, not search engines. If you find yourself stuffing your site with keywords, you have lost the plot. Never is this truer than in the area of image alt tags.

The original purpose of alt tags was twofold: to allow text-browser users to "see" images, and to help partially sighted or blind users to "read" images using, for example, screen-reader software. The use of text browsers (or HTML browsers with the images turned off) has now fallen to negligible levels following the widespread penetration of broad-band. However, disabled users still make use of screen readers and need accurate descriptions of pictures in order to make full sense of a web page.

Generally, in these days of clean, fresh Web 2.0 design, I would keep the use of images to an absolute minimum on your site (and only to make it visually appealing). Where you do use images, ensure that the following recommendations are met:

- ✧ Every image must have an alt tag, with the exception of spacer images (having alt text for the latter is very irritating for disabled users).
- ✧ The alt tag should faithfully describe the image concerned; the opportunity to include your keyphrases should not be lost, but do not simply stuff the tag with keywords.

Say, for example, that your image is of two people shaking hands and this is meant to symbolize "collaboration solutions" (one of your keyphrases and the topic of your page). Suitable alt text might be: "Two people shaking hands, symbolizing collaboration solutions from ABC company."

Note that there is no need to say "image of" at the start of your description. Screen-reader software tells the user of the existence of an image before reading them the alt text. As such, if you included "image of," the screen reader would read back something like "image of image of." Don't annoy your disabled users by failing to understand this key point.

FORUM TOOLS HTML validators are very useful for spotting missing alt tags, although they can be very frustrating, like very strict school-teachers who always find "room for improvement" in your end-of-term report! On the forum (www.seo-expert-services.co.uk) I provide a list of suitable validators. For the purposes of this illustration, pay a visit to the W3 Markup Validation tool (currently at http://validator.w3.org/).

Enter your URLs in turn and click on the accessibility tab in the results. From here you can see how many missing alt tags you have and drill down to which images are missing them. Make your fixes and revalidate until you are happy.

Internal links

More SEO value is ascribed to internal links (with good anchor text) than many people seem to realize. I am often surprised at how many companies spend ages trying to secure inbound links from other sites (more on this later, page 132) but have no decent, keyword-rich navigation within their own site (where, after all, everything is under their control). We have already discussed breadcrumb trails (an important part of the internal link process). I am now going to consider your main navigation elements.

How you implement your navigation is really up to you (and will depend much more on your design preferences than on SEO). However, usability studies have shown time and time again that the vast majority of people prefer so-called split-menu navigation, where tabs across the top bar of the page are used for navigating to sections, and link boxes in the lefthand bar navigate around the categories and content pages below.

The main point I want to make, however, is that you should always use real text in your navigation elements rather than images. In these days of cascading style sheets (where almost anything is possible, in terms of styling), there is really no excuse for missing the opportunity for further use of keyword-rich anchor text in your links.

In-context links are internal links that appear in the middle of your page. In a section or category page, you might attach links to the heading fields (so that people can click on them to access the next level down in the hierarchy). More generally, you might link keyphrases, where they appear in the body text, to the content pages most relevant to them. My advice is to do this wherever possible but always in moderation, If every other word group is a link, your page will start to look silly. Done well, however, links aid navigation for the user and search engine alike.

And don't neglect the simple things on your web pages. Add a <u>feedback form</u> so that customers can give you ideas on how to improve the site. Give them a <u>mailto:</u> link they can use to send an email to a friend recommending your site, and use some Javascript to create an <u>add to favourites</u> link, so people can more easily bookmark your site.

Outbound links

There are two competing views of how to determine authority in the world of search. Google, as we shall see later, look at the number of inbound links a site receives. Ask.com, by contrast, tends to look more at the number of outbound links from a site. Borrowing from the wheel analogy, I call this the "hub vs. spoke" debate. Ask tends to believe that a site with a lot of outbound links on a particular topic is a hub of useful information and resources. Google, by contrast, tends to look for the most useful spoke (i.e., the page most people end up on eventually), although its position on this may be changing.

More generally, Google has always tracked "related sites." You can see what Google pairs you with by typing site:yourdomain.com into the query box, then clicking on the "similar sites" link from the result. What sort of company are you keeping? You may be somewhat confused by the sites you see there, but don't worry too much. The key point is that some of them are based on your outbound links.

A more interesting way to explore interrelationships is to pay a visit to the visually stunning kartoo.com. Try searching on your business name to see how your site relates (in keyword terms) to your competitors.

I generally recommend that clients do consider linking out from their site (where appropriate) to other high-quality websites that are on a similar topic or theme to their own. Generally, you should target sites with a PageRank PR7 or better for best effect. Use keyword-rich links to make the connection. Avoid placing such links on "money pages" or

URL rewrite	http://www.chambersprint.com/business-printing/business-cards/business-card-printing.html
\<title\> tag	Chambers > Business Printing > Online Business Card Printing – Ranges
Meta description tag	Online Business Card Printing services from Chambers of Boise. We offer short print run, full color business card printing on luxury business cards and cheap business cards
Meta keyword tag	online,business card printing,luxury business cards,cheap business cards,short print runs,business card design,laminated business cards,business card printing services,cheap business cards,custom business cards,business cards Boise,budget business cards,discount business cards
Breadcrumb trail	Chambers Business Printing » Business Printing » Business Cards – Business Cards to suit all budgets
\<h1\> tag	**Online Business Card Printing from Chambers**
Body text paragraph	At Chambers Print we understand that, when you need business print services, you normally need fast, full color printing at a reasonable price! If you wish, you can upload your own artwork or business logo. Simply select a template from our wide selection, upload the image and preview the design online before you buy!
	IMAGE Alt tag: Business card Range from Chambers Print
\<h1\> tag	**Business Cards to suit all budgets, in short print runs**
Body text paragraph	Whether you are looking for premium business cards (from our luxury business card range) or discount business cards to suit a tight budget, we can deliver within 48 hours and in short print runs if required (with no minimum order quantity). We can even make you CD business cards or business card magnets, for when you need to stand out from the crowd!
\<h1\> tag	**Browse our Business Card Ranges**
\<h2\> tags defined as links	» Luxury Business Cards » Cheap Business Cards » CD-Rom Business Cards » Business Card Magnets
\<h1\> tag	**Know what you want?**
\<h2\> tag defined as a link	Upload your own artwork and print your business cards now »
Footer	Site Map	Help	Accessibility	Terms of Use	Privacy Policy Copyright 2007 Chambers Business Print

anywhere else where an exit could prove fatal to a key customer journey. Don't overdo it, but do do a bit of it.

You are probably wondering at this point what happened to Brad. I have left him alone for a while because I wanted to give you one single example that demonstrates the whole page structure.

> Opposite is an extract from Brad's content plan – something I rec-ommend to all my clients. Essentially, the copy for each and every page, with mark-up annotations, is prepared prior to web develop-ment in a wordprocessing file and sent to the web developers. This way, there is no excuse for sloppy errors.

3.3 Asset optimization

You are now armed with everything you need to construct decent, well-optimized HTML pages. Having primed your pages, you should also consider optimization of the other assets found on your web server.

Web designers tend to refer to all the HTML files on a web server as "pages" and all the other files on a web server as "assets." As such, assets include picture files (.jpg, .gif, .png, etc.), documents (.doc, .pdf), spreadsheets (.xls), presentations (.ppt), videos (.avi, etc.), and more. I have covered image files in the "priming your pages" section above (page 110). In this section, I focus on Microsoft Office and PDF files, and videos.

Documents and spreadsheets

Try typing "intranet communications plan" into Google. One of the top results should be a work of mine from the "Dig For Victory" Intranet Portal Guide site. The document will appear in the SERPs as follows:

[DOC] <u>Intranet Portal Guide – Project Communications</u>
File Format: Microsoft Word – View as HTML
Future exploitation projects will build our Intranet capabilities towards world class, to provide a context for .... Summary of the COMMUNICATION PLAN ...
www.viney.com/DFV/pub/commplan.doc

Use right-click, save-target-as to download the file to your PC, then open the document in Microsoft Word. Use the menu option File – Properties to open up the properties dialogue, then click on the "Summary" tab. The data is as follows:

  ✧ Title: Intranet Portal Guide – Project Communications
  ✧ Subject: Communications Plan
  ✧ Keywords: intranet,corporate,portal,communications,plan

Notice anything? The text Google used for the link in the SERPs was the title field from the properties meta data. The description field was drawn from the body of the document. The same principle works for Excel files, PowerPoint presentations, and Adobe PDFs.

I recommend revisiting all of the Office and PDF files you have on your web servers and properly recoding your meta data to add a meaningful title, add keywords, and, if you can, change the filename of your asset to include your keywords. For example, intranet-communications-plan.doc would have been better than commplan.doc.

Incidentally, if there are any documents that you don't want people to find in a search, simply put these files in a directory called "Private" and prevent Google from indexing the directory using the robots.txt commands I explained earlier (page 57).

Video optimization

Search engine optimization for video is one of the most exciting challenges in the field, since Google has recently started giving videos much greater prominence in regular search results. Getting it right is remarkably simple, and in many ways is simply an extension of the principles we have seen for optimizing Microsoft Office and PDF files.

First of all, you need to prepare your video files properly. Locate the video file in Windows Explorer and make sure the file is not set to read only, then right-click on the video's icon to access properties. Rename the file to a keyword-rich alternative. Use hyphenated keyphrases (e.g. business-cards-from-chambers.avi). Next, right-click again and access the "Summary" tab. Add a keyword-rich title (e.g. Business Cards from Chambers Print) and some useful keywords.

Google Video supports the upload of .avi, .mpg, Quicktime, and Windows Media files (so nearly all the extensions you are used to). The frame rate should be above 12 frames per second and the bit rate should be above 260kbps. Google will crop your video to fit within a 4:3 frame and display it at 320×240 resolution using Macromedia Flash. As such, if you are preparing your video from scratch, try to use the 4:3 aspect ratio to make sure it plays the way you want and avoid arbitrary "letterbox" cropping issues.

There are two ways to get your videos onto Google Video. If your video file is under 100MB, the easiest and fastest way to upload it is to use Google's web-based uploader (at https://upload.video.google.com/). If your video is over 100MB or you'd like to upload multiple files at once, the Google Video Uploader client software is your best bet (currently at https://upload.video.google.com/video_instructions.html). As a rough guide, keeping your video to 4.5 minutes or less should make the whole process a lot easier.

If you upload from the web-based interface, you can specify up front the title, description, genre, and language of the file. For the title field, simply repeat (perhaps at greater length) the title you used for the file properties dialogue. For the description, follow the same principles we covered in the meta-description tag section (see page 103). Select an appropriate genre (e.g., "business"), set access to public, and click to upload your video.

Once your video is up on Google (or YouTube), you can obtain code to insert the video into your web page. Usefully, this means that Google is hosting and serving the video rather than you (saving on your computing power and bandwidth charges).

This is the Wild West frontier of SEO, so enjoy yourself. You could find this to be your quickest route into the top 10 (at least for the time being, until the spammers get hold of it). Put in a few inbound links to your video, get friends and colleagues to vote for it on Google Video, and see what happens. You might surprise yourself.

3.4 Manipulating snippets and SERPs

SERPs manipulation is the (rather advanced) art of optimizing how your site appears in Google's search engine results pages (SERPs). The overall entry (or entries) is, at best, a superb call to action that will draw the visitor's eye and encourage click-throughs. Before we explore this in greater depth, it is first necessary to understand a little about how Google formats its SERPs.

How Google formats results

Previously, we have seen how Google finds pages and how it indexes them. In the next step we learn how Google orders (or ranks) results for any given search query (the very heart of SEO). Here I cover the end result: the formatting of those query results.

Try a search for "Panasonic TVs" on Google. You will note that the first block of results (three of them) at the top of the page are sponsored results and that a further nine sponsored results appear down the righthand side. Underneath the first three sponsored results is a OneBox insertion (in this case "product search"), which gives <u>integrated results</u> from Google Product Search. For now I want to focus on the first ten <u>organic search</u> results (from the Google index) that make up the rest of the page.

The design of Google's results pages is based on years of trial and error – and extensive research. However, the very fact that only ten organic results are served on each page (when coupled with the task of scrolling down and surfers' natural impatience) means that top rankings draw more than their fair share of searches. The analysis in the following table is based on research by OneUp.com.

Google organic search position	For 1,000 searches on a typical keyword, this many clicks go to the sites in that position	Percentage
1–11	478	48%
11–20	361	36%
21–30	122	12%
31+	39	4%
Total	1,000	100%

The implications of this analysis should not be lost on you: 84% of searchers never make it beyond page two of the organic results and 96% never go beyond page three. They are, in fact, much more likely to try a different search than to continue laboriously down the results.

However, the layout of the page has some further interesting characteristics to surprise you with. Try searching for "Google heat analysis" or "Google eyeball analysis" in Google Image Search. You will find numerous references to the so-called <u>F-pattern</u>, which describes how users scan the Google results (with their eyes) when taking in a results page. People tend to track across titles from left to right, beginning at the top left of the page. They then drop down to the next title and do the same. With each title, they track slightly less to the right, until by the time they are "below the fold" of the page (i.e., where they have to scroll down to read further), very few are still looking at the page. In heat analysis, this resembles an F-shape.

Research from enquiro.com, leaders in this field, suggests the following pattern in eyeball visibility (for each result on any given search results page):

Position on page	Visibility	Position on page	Visibility
1	100%	6	50%
2	100%	7	50%
3	100%	8	30%
4	85%	9	30%
5	60%	10	20%

Would it surprise you to learn, therefore, that it is probably better to be ranked number 11 than number 10 in Google? You may have noticed from the first table that 100% - 48% = 52% of users make it to at least the top of page two. As such, 20% × 100% = 20% of users properly scan position 10 but 100% × 52% = 52% of users properly scan position 11 (which is at the top of page two of the results). Without full, organic click-through analysis from Google this is difficult to test, but it is an interesting hypothesis nonetheless.

So what about <u>paid results</u>? Further research has indicated that on average, 65% of users click on the organic listings and 35% use the paid or sponsored listings. Generally, positions 1, 4, and 8 in the sponsored results are the most highly sought after by those in the know. Again, eyeball analysis indicates that position 1 is where the eye most often starts scanning, position 4 is where the eye stops for a moment at the end of the top of the F, and position 8 is where the eye goes when looking to scroll down through the search results.

Indented results

Now for a quick introduction to something I call the Holy Grail of SEO with respect to SERPs: indented results. When Google finds multiple results from the same website (for any given search query) the most important result is listed first, with another relevant page from that site indented below it. A key point is that only 10 results will be displayed on any given results page, including any indents. So if you have a top 10 result – with one additional page indented – you have essentially secured two links (or 20% of all the links on the page). Later (page 150) I will show you how to use deep links to achieve this outcome – and work wonders for your site traffic.

SiteLinks

If indented links are the Holy Grail, then SiteLinks are the Ark of the Covenant and the Turin Shroud rolled into one. Try putting "autoglass" into Google. The first result will be for Autoglass, a UK-based windscreen-repair service. You will note that there are no fewer than five SiteLinks included below the main search result, linking the user to different parts of the Autoglass site. SiteLinks are completely automated but seem to occur only when, for the search query used:

- ✦ The site is ranked number one in the SERPs.
- ✦ The site has significantly more inbound links (with that search term in the link anchor text) than any other site.
- ✦ The site has a well-structured (and easily crawled) sitemap.
- ✦ The vast majority of click-throughs for that search term go to this site.

Normally, the sites that fair best with SiteLinks are those for well-known brands and with only one domain for their content.

Snippets

Each of the 10 results on the page comprises the search result link and the search snippet. The link (as I have already explained, page 103) equates to the title of your page, truncated to 63 characters or the last complete word (whichever is the shorter). The snippet is more complex, compiled by Google from the meta-description tag, relevant on-page text, and (where available) data from the Open Directory Project (www.dmoz.org, the largest human-edited directory of the web). The title and description in the SERPs together comprise a "call to action" for the searcher, enticing them to click on the link. As such, it is vital to get your snippet working well for the most likely search combinations.

The key point with snippets is all about the difference between "search marketing" and "search engine optimization." The former is concerned with the marketing message that goes out to the user, while the latter is concerned simply with positions in the rankings. While the snippet in general (and the description meta tag in particular) may be of limited significance in SEO, it is all important for search marketing, because of its role in getting users to click through to your pages.

So how does Google compile a snippet? Well, the first thing to realize is that it will display a different snippet for each search query entered. What the results formatting program does is look through the indexed text from your page, searching (generally) for the first and next/last appearance of the search query text. As your description tag is at the beginning of the indexed text, it comes to it first. If the entire search phrase is only found in the description tag, you may find that it is used to compile the entire snippet. If, however, the search query (or part of it) is repeated at least once elsewhere on your page, Google may splice together a bit of text from your tag and a bit of text from your page, separating the two with an ellipsis (...) to indicate intentionally omitted words.

If Google struggles to find the query text anywhere on your page, it may use data drawn from either the Open Directory Project or your

Yahoo! directory listing. This does cause some webmasters consternation, as directory listings are edited by someone else (and the webmaster thus loses control of the message). I will look at this interesting phenomenon first.

Try putting "scuba dive" into Google. The number one result will still be www.padi.com when you read this (I hope, or this example is not going to work too well):

> <u>PADI – The Way the World Learns to Dive. Find out how, why and ...</u>
> The largest and most recognized diving organization around the
> world with courses ranging from Snorkeling to Course Director.

PADI has a very visual homepage, so its body text is minimal. The title and description tag (used by PADI at time of writing) are identical: "PADI – The Way the World Learns to Dive. Find out how, why and where to dive."

Google uses PADI's title tag (as it contains the word "dive" at least), but where did it get that snippet from? These words appear nowhere on the PADI page. For your answer, go to the Open Directory Project (www.dmoz.org) and navigate down through Recreation > Outdoors > Scuba diving > Organizations > Training agencies. Near the bottom of the page, you will find the entry for PADI:

> ODP Link: PADI – Professional Association of Diving Instructors
> ODP Description: The largest and most recognized diving organization around the world with courses ranging from Snorkeling to Course Director.

Does this description look familiar? This is the exact text that Google uses for its snippet, having found nothing on the PADI page to text match. Now for the really interesting part. Try "scuba diving" in Google and, again, PADI should show up near the top:

PADI – Professional Association of Diving Instructors
The largest and most recognized diving organization around the
world with courses ranging from Snorkeling to Course Director.

Notice how the title tag is now being taken from the ODP data too? This
is because the word "dive" is in the title on PADI's site but not "diving."

The sharper among you will have noticed the really important
learning point from this (to which we will return in our next section):
How come PADI ranks number one for a phrase that doesn't appear
anywhere on its homepage? A good question. However, for now just log
the fact that Google uses quality directories as a last resort in text-matching snippets.

So what if you don't like your ODP or Yahoo! listing? After all, the
whole nature of your site or business may have changed in the last few
years (since your directory entry was first submitted) and getting an
update to such listings can be a struggle. Fortunately, there is now a way
to tell Google and Yahoo! to ignore these entries when compiling snippets, using these two meta tags between your <head> tags:

```
<meta name="robots" content="noodp" />
<meta name="robots" content="noydir" />
```

The first of these tags tells all robots not to use ODP content and the
latter tells them not to use Yahoo! directory content. For efficiency, you
can combine the two into a single tag using the following:

```
<meta name="robots" content="noodp,noydir" />
```

Right, now that's out of the way, let's assume you want to control your
own meta description and focus on the more interesting question of how
to manipulate snippet construction to your advantage. The advice I am
about to give does not always work, so you may have to use trial and
error to find the right solution.

Try a search on google.co.uk for "sharepoint 2007 consulting."
Hopefully the homepage of Alchemy (one of the businesses I work with)
will still be near the top of the results. The search result (unless I have
played with it again recently) should look like this:

Overview – from Alchemy (Intranet Portal & SharePoint
Consultants)
Intranet Portal Delivery from SharePoint 2007 consultants,
Alchemy eBusiness Consulting... Request a proposal for SharePoint
2007 Consulting.

Not bad, eh? Now try "sharepoint 2007 specialists" and you should get
the following:

Overview – from Alchemy (Intranet Portal & SharePoint
Consultants)
As SharePoint 2007 specialists, we deliver portals for large UK busi-
nesses... Request a proposal for SharePoint 2007 Consulting.

Snippet manipulation is fraught with challenges. However, in general the
best way to achieve good results is to follow these principles:

- ✧ Ensure that your description tag contains approximately 24–26
  words overall, split into two sentences of roughly equal length.
  Do not exceed 180 characters (including spaces) and aim,
  ideally, for no more than 160.
- ✧ Both sentences in the description tag should introduce your
  business, only in different ways (so that if Google serves the
  whole description tag as a snippet it will not look too strange).
- ✧ Ideally, each sentence will contain one of your top two three-
  word keyphrases for the page in question (in Alchemy's case
  "SharePoint 2007 specialists" or "SharePoint 2007
  consultants").

✧ Ensure that the very final paragraph of your body text – i.e., immediately prior to any footer text in your HTML file – contains fewer characters than the shortest of your two description sentences, and at least the stem of your most important keyphrase (in this case "SharePoint 2007"). Avoid overuse of this phrase elsewhere on the page (unless you are operating in a very competitive environment) or you will lose control over the snippet.

✧ This body-text sentence should be between six and nine words in length and contain a clear call to action for the user (relevant to this page).

With a bit of luck (and some experimentation), Google will splice together one sentence from your description tag with the last sentence from your body text. The result will be a snippet that a search marketer would be proud of! Keep trying different combinations (a new one every time you are crawled) until you are happy with the snippet you find on Google.

Remember, Google will display a different snippet in its results pages for each search query used. For this reason, it's impossible to control completely what will show up, as you have no way of knowing every single keyword phrase that someone might use to find your site.

Finally, if you are operating in a very competitive sector where one search phrase is used much more often than another, then ensure that this phrase is used in both sentences of your meta-description tag (and that the two sentences together create a great introduction and call to action). This should ensure that Google uses your meta tag in its entirety to serve the snippet.

For his home page, Brad opts for the following meta-description tag of 26 words and 184 characters in all (including spaces). This is a little longer than I would like, but then Brad has a lot to cram into a small space:

Business Cards and Business Printing services from Chambers Print of Boise, Idaho. We offer online business card printing, letterheads, compliment slips, printed address labels & more.

Near the footer of his page, Brad includes the following call-to-action sentence:

Upload your own artwork and print your business cards now.

After some further experimentation, Brad achieves the results he was hoping for, both for his homepage and his other pages.

Step 4: Landing the links

So far, you have learnt how to court the crawl, find the phrases that pay, and prime your pages. Now take a deep breath. Everything you have discovered so far barely scrapes the surface of what is necessary to rank well on Google. Yes, that's right. All the keyword research, site set-up, and on-page copywriting in the world only gets you to the starting line in the race you still need to run. Think of yourself as a raw athlete, fit and physically well prepared, but still to prove yourself, and – above all else – still unknown to the world. Or, to return to our painting analogy, you may have primed your walls perfectly (flat, smooth, and clean), but until you have started painting the job isn't really even begun, let alone finished.

If on-page SEO is all about the tools and techniques you can use on web server assets that are fully under your control, off-page SEO is all about getting other webmasters to point (or link) their users to your site – what I call landing the links. This is so important because of how Google ranks pages with otherwise similar relevance.

As you will now discover, **the route to good Google ranking is to get a high quantity and quality of links to your pages from important, relevant, and reliable sources.**

4.1 How Google ranks

All the best businesses start in garages and all the best search engines start on university campuses. It really is true. At its outset, Google was the research project (nicknamed "BackRub") of two Stanford PhD students: Michigan-born Larry Page and Russian Sergey Brin. At the time there were already many successful search engines, with Altavista the market leader. While everyone else was focused on size and quantity (how to index all of the fast-growing web), Page was obsessed by quality (how to rank the most relevant pages near the top of your results).

In his original thesis research, Page hypothesized that any link from one site to another was akin to an academic citation; the description (or anchor text) attached to that link was like an annotation. If one could identify the sites most cited for any given annotated subject, one could establish a pecking order of significance for any given subject area.

What particularly fascinated Page was what he saw as a fundamental weakness in Tim Berners-Lee's original design for the web; namely, that it was possible to see easily what any site was linking to, but very hard (if not impossible) to see the sites linking back. BackRub sought to catalogue all the links on the web and, through doing so, establish which sites had the most "authority" overall and on any given topic. Page insists that it was never his intention at this point to create a search engine. However, intellectual curiosity drove him forward into the creation of a new kind of crawler, based on a link-ranking system; the first (and still best) of its kind.

PageRank: What Google deems important

The heart of the Google algorithm is the very same link-based system developed at Stanford and is called <u>PageRank</u> (after Larry Page, its inventor, rather than after the pages themselves). Google explains PageRank in the following way:

> PageRank relies on the uniquely democratic nature of the web
> by using its vast link structure as an indicator of an individual
> page's value. In essence, Google interprets a link from page A
> to page B as a vote, by page A, for page B...

In a sense, then, PageRank is like a giant electronic voting system. The page that gets the most votes gets awarded the highest PageRank (on a scale of 0–10). So, grossly oversimplifying, simple importance is determined by link quantity.

This is not the whole story, however. Google goes on to explain:

Google looks at considerably more than the sheer volume of votes, or links a page receives; for example, it also analyzes the page that casts the vote. Votes cast by pages that are themselves "important" weigh more heavily and help to make other pages "important." Using these and other factors, Google provides its views on pages' relative importance.

To continue the voting analogy, Google is not a first-past-the-post system. Every vote is not equal. If you get a vote from another site that has already garnered many votes of its own, this will carry a greater weighting than a vote from a relative unknown. So, to complete the picture, relative importance (or PageRank) is determined by both link quantity and link source importance. I explore PageRank in more detail in the tracking and tuning section (page 229).

Text matching: What Google deems relevant

Ok, let's assume you have cracked relative importance and have a PageRank of 10. Now your page ranks number one on Google for every single related search undertaken by a user, right? Wrong!

The easiest way to illustrate this is by means of an example. I know that the Guggenheim Museum in New York is a relatively important art gallery, as it is cited as such by many important sources. However, the Guggenheim focuses on modern art, so if I were searching for seventeenth-century landscapes I would be unlikely to find its content relevant to my search.

If, however, I were searching for the art of Piet Mondrian, then Guggenheim's importance – when combined with its relevance to Mondrian and his work – should absolutely ensure that it appears near the top of the rankings. Try the search "Piet Mondrian" in Google or Yahoo! and you will see that the Guggenheim does indeed feature in the top 10 (although MSN and Ask notably fail to include it there). So how do the people at Google do this? Well, as they themselves put it, the search engine:

goes far beyond the number of times a term appears on a page and examines dozens of aspects of the page's content (and the content of the pages linking to it) to determine if it's a good match for your query.

In short, the Guggenheim page about Piet Mondrian ranks so well because many sites about the artist (with lots of text containing the word Mondrian) link to the Guggenheim, often with Mondrian in the link text. See for example www.pietmondrian.org and http://en.wikipedia. org/wiki/Piet_Mondrian.

This sophisticated process is known as <u>text matching</u>. From my years of SEO experience, the most important of all these text-matching factors is link quality, where as many as possible of the links to your pages use your phrases that pay in their anchor text. The closer the anchor text is to your desired keyphrases, the greater the link quality will be. In the next section I will prove to you just how important link quality is (page 132).

TrustRank: What Google deems reliable

The more established a site or its links are, the more Google appears to assign "trust" and weighting in its algorithm, often known as <u>TrustRank</u>. Links from well-established sites like the Yahoo! directory, the Open Directory Project, .gov, .edu, and other sites established in the earliest days of the web carry greater source reliability and weighting in the ranking of your site.

You can find out the age of a web domain (and a whole host of other useful facts) by paying a visit to a decent <u>Whois tool</u>. On my forum I list a selection of the best, but for the purposes of this illustration, pay a visit to Domain Tools (http://whois.domaintools.com). Put in the URL you want to investigate like this:

http://whois.domaintools.com/yourdomain.com

The tool returns basic page information, indexed data (from the Open Directory Project and Wikipedia), and server data (including the country in which the IP is based). It also provides registrar data and the full Whois record (including the date on which the domain was first registered).

The recipe

So, to summarize, today's overall Google algorithm combines relative importance, relevance, and reliability to determine the overall significance of a page for any given search. The PageRank algorithm determines the relative importance of all pages, using link quantity and source importance as the main criteria. The TrustRank algorithm determines source reliability, mainly using age as a proxy. The Text Matching algorithm determines the relevance of both site and source, using link quality and other related factors. These three algorithms work in tandem with numerous spam filters to effortlessly deliver (in milliseconds) fantastic search results for just about any query from Aardvarks to Zanzibar.

This simple section is actually the pivot of this entire book. Everything before now has been building up to this recipe and everything that follows is the cooking instructions. It sounds pretty simple, doesn't it? Hardly cordon bleu! However, not everyone knows how to cook, and few know the right recipe. More importantly, very few people have the determination to stay the cookery course and put in the hard hours required to become a really good chef. You will be different - you will succeed!

4.2 Off-page optimization

Off-page SEO is the heart and soul of a successful optimization campaign and comprises all the tools and techniques you need to get other site owners to rate your site. All of these techniques together deliver a large quantity of high-quality links to your site from important, reliable, and relevant sources.

This section is the longest in the book because it is the most important. Your site may be full of superb and relevant content and your pages may be the best primed of any site in your niche, but if no one knows of your existence and no one has cited you as an authoritative source, then why should Google take any notice?

Remember how PADI ranked in the top 10 on Google for both "scuba diving" and "scuba dive" without containing either phrase on its homepage? That alone might have been proof enough of the importance of off-page inbound links. However, some of you will still assume that, as PADI is the official organization for scuba divers, there must be other content on its whole site (from an on-page perspective) that pushes it to the top.

Think again, doubting Thomases. I have saved up a really special example for you to dispel any lingering skepticism. Try typing "click here" into Google. This is a number one result that I do not expect to change any time soon. The top position goes to the Adobe Acrobat Reader download page. Adobe is not a professional society for clickers. The page does not contain the words "click here" (or anything remotely like it) and nor does the rest of the Adobe site. So how is this almost magical result achieved? The answer is simple: hundreds of thousands of pages linking to this one with the phrase:

Click here to download Adobe Acrobat Reader.

So there you are: proof positive that a large number of high-quality links, described using keyword-rich anchor text, is (at least for now) the crucial and deciding factor in strong Google rankings.

In this section I will walk you through a large number of different off-page techniques. However (and for the avoidance of confusion), all of them have just one aim: to acquire more and better inbound links than the pages of your competitors.

How many links do I need?

Your inbound link-building activities fall into two groups: active and passive. The former involves you actively contacting other sites to submit or request a link. The latter involves link baiting, where you create attractive content and invite others (in a more passive way) to link back to it.

For sufficient quantity and quality, I recommend that you actively build at least 250 and not more than 750 unique inbound links, containing your phrases that pay in the anchor text. By unique, I mean that you only count one link per domain (so 25 links from different pages on www.otherdomain1.com only count as one link).

To ensure source importance, target sites that have been established at least three years (and preferably more than seven) and that carry a homepage PageRank of at least PR3 (and ideally PR5 or more). To ensure source relevance, target pages where possible that have similar content to your own or operate in the same niche.

If your niche is very competitive by all means build more links, but avoid actively building more than 1,500 links yourself. You can have too many links. There are several examples of what I call "superoveroptimized" sites that have fallen back through the rankings. I won't name them here (for legal among other reasons) but take my word for it. The point is that there is a very fine line between seeking authority and spamming Google.

While there is no hard-and-fast ceiling, if you are getting up into the 15,000+ zone for inbound links then you may be putting yourself at risk. It's not just the absolute number but also the speed with which links are acquired and the pattern of those links. Anything that looks too good to be true generally is.

I won't go as far as to say that rapid link building will inevitably end in disaster (as there will always be sites that get away with this). However, there is a much more important reason not to go over the top: your own time. As I have said before in this book, your time is better spent running your business than building links all day and night.

Instead, once you have your 250–750 baseline of inbound links in place, focus thereafter on passive techniques that bait others into linking to you (without being asked).

Planning and preparation

Turn your mind back to your phrases that pay. From your keyword analysis you created a "site-wide" and "deep phrase" list, and weighted those phrases for deployment. Site-wide phrases were the 3–5 two-word and 4–6 three-word phrases that had the highest keyword weighting on your A list. The rest were your deep phrases. As I said earlier, site-wide phrases will be used to optimize your homepage and deep phrases to target individual sections, categories, or content pages.

Link-building tracking tool

To plan your active inbound link campaign, create a workbook in Excel or similar software with two spreadsheets. The first spreadsheet should be called "Tracking" and should have seven columns:

A – Keyphrase
B – Weighting in % (column should total 100%)
C – Total number of links in campaign (e.g., 250)
D – Number of links (B × C)
E – Requested/submitted
F – Accepted
G – Percentage complete

The second spreadsheet should be called "Requests" and should have eight columns:

A – Site name
B – External URL

C – Request type
D – Requested anchor text
E – Request date
F – Completed (Y/N)
G – Actual anchor text
H – Notes

This workbook will be used to track the progress of your active link campaign and to log and chase individual link requests made to other site
owners.

Perhaps the easiest way to illustrate this is to turn once again to
Chambers Business Printing.

> Brad decides to undertake an initial, active link-building campaign
> to gain 250 links. To achieve this number of accepted links, he
> decides to make 350 requests (i.e., 250 × 140%) to allow for a
> number of failures. He also decides to round up the number of
> requests for each keyphrase to a minimum of five and reduce the
> number of links for his main phrase "business cards" accordingly to
> bring the total back to 350.
>
> After two months Brad reviews his progress, using his link-
> tracking spreadsheet. Opposite is a short extract from that spread-
> sheet (using the same example keyphrases we saw earlier).
>
> Brad is pleased to note that he has hit his target of 250
> accepted requests (he actually has 252). He has checked these links
> either manually or using Yahoo! Site Explorer and confirmed the
> sites' existence.

You will notice that Brad's distribution in the example above is heavily
skewed in favor of the phrase "business cards." This is actually fairly
unusual. First, I have only shown you an extract from Brad's list; if we
had included all his other phrases, the weight attached to each would
have fallen (and other phrases like "letterhead printing" would have

Keyphrase	Weight %	Total links	Target links	No. of requests	No. accepted	% complete
Business cards	90.05	250	223	283	198	70.2
Business card printing	7.74	250	20	27	22	81.5
Business printing	1.18	250	4	5	4	66.7
Online business card printing	0.26	250	1	5	5	100.0
Business card printing services	0.18	250	1	5	4	80.0
Business card printing service	0.16	250	1	5	3	60.0
Color business card printing	0.15	250	1	5	5	100.0
Full color business card printing	0.17	250	1	5	4	80.0
Cheap business card printing	0.06	250	1	5	3	60.0
Business card printing company	0.03	250	1	5	4	80.0
Total	100	250	250	350	252	72.0

risen up the list). Secondly, Brad's sector is unusually uncompetitive, with "business cards" having a very high KOI score. I would expect your outcome to be more balanced. However, you will still find, like Brad, that there are one or two phrases that dominate the rest in your weighting (due in part to the operation of the long tail that I explained earlier). Do not be afraid to set a minimum of five or more for every deep-phrase link and reduce your top phrases accordingly.

Main links and deep links

You may have heard the phrase deep links before and wondered what it means. In simple terms, deep links are links from other sites to internal pages on your site (for example http://www.yourdomain/section1/cate-gory2/page3.html). Main links, by contrast, are links to the homepage of your site.

Generally, you want 5–20% of your actively built links to be deep links, using your deep phrases as the anchor text. The balance of your links will be main links to your homepage, using site-wide phrases as the anchor text. Your deep-link percentage will be near the top of this 5–20% range if your long tail is pretty flat (with primary keyphrases not dominating) and near the bottom of this range if your curve is more like Brad's.

Now you have a plan for your active link building, it is time to introduce you to all the ethical link-building strategies at your disposal. I will move from the more active to the more passive routes, punctuating each explanation with forum tools and resources.

Reciprocal link exchange

Ever since high-street shops first started to appear, it has been common practice for business owners to exchange advertisements, postcards and flyers, cross-promoting one another's businesses (these are often stuck on walls or shop-front windows). Many also actively recommend complementary services from other businesses with which they have a relationship. For example, a wedding-venue provider might recommend a wedding caterer with whom they have worked successfully in the past.

Similarly, on the web it has been common practice for years to exchange links between webmasters. Witness the pages called linkpartners.html or web-resources.html. Some webmasters go further and build huge link directories off the back of their sites, with outbound links to literally hundreds of partners. Some of these directories are even built using dedicated link-building scripts that semi-automate the process.

You may have seen on some forums that reciprocal link building is a waste of time because Google now ignores such links. This is simply not true – all links do count in the end. However, it is true that reciprocal links are worth less than they used to be, as Google deflates the value of such links in computing your rankings. As such, while reciprocal link building can be a useful part of the active link-building toolset, it is by no means the most important club in your bag, more of a six iron than a driver.

Personally, I am not a fan of automated link directory-building software, as it smacks of desperation and creates ugly, spammy pages deep in your site. However, I do recommend to clients the use of <u>membership-only link exchanges</u>. Such services, at their best, are highly ethical and seek to matchmake webmasters with websites in the same topic area. By exchanging links with webmasters operating sites complementary to your own, you can improve the overall relevance of your site to those searching for your chosen products, services, or information.

FORUM TOOLS On the forum (www.seo-expert-services.co.uk) I list a number of reciprocal link-building resources, with a focus on membership-only services. For the purposes of this section I will use Link Metro as an example.

Visit www.linkmetro.com and register for the service. You enter your full name, login details, and email address as normal. You then add a site URL and the site title and description that you would like people to use when linking to you. Most importantly, you also enter a category into which you feel your site fits. Brad, for example, would select Business & Industry > Printing.

Once accepted into the community, you can either actively initiate linking requests with other webmasters (typically in your category) or passively wait for others to make offers to you. You could do a bit of both.

Do be ready to reject more link requests than you receive, as many of the requests you get will be unsuitable. Do investigate the website of anyone requesting a link and look at the existing links that site already has (using Yahoo! Site Explorer). Reject anything off topic and requests from sites with (long-term) PR0 homepages or spammy domain names. Not all the webmasters in such communities are ethical. Be careful of the company you keep and only exchange links with sites you would wish to visit yourself.

In addition to using membership services, you may also want to initiate some linking requests by email. Personally, I would keep such requests to a minimum, as they are time consuming to prepare, dispatch, track, and act on. The success rate is also typically poor. If you must send out reciprocal link requests to other sites, here is my recommended approach (and etiquette):

- ✧ <u>Only seek links with related sites</u>. The less relevant your target site is, the less likely it is that the webmaster will accept your request. Don't waste your time and don't waste theirs. My inbox is full of such requests and it drives me mad.
- ✧ <u>Begin by putting a link to their site on your own site first</u>. This removes any doubt in the mind of the recipient about whether you will keep your end of the bargain or not.
- ✧ <u>Look for a contact form on the site</u> (which might have a "request link" checkbox) or a link you can click to exchange links. If the webmaster is inviting link exchange, there is a high likelihood they will accept a request.
- ✧ <u>Make sure that your note is well written</u> and personalized to the recipient. If it reads like junk mail, it is likely to be treated as such.
- ✧ <u>Make the active part of your request a polite one</u>. Try congratulating the webmaster on an excellent site, highlighting the complementary nature of your own site, pointing out that you have already linked to their site, and politely inviting them to reciprocate.
- ✧ <u>Be specific in your note</u> about what link – and keyword-rich link text – you would like them to use. Where possible, send them the HTML code readymade, so they don't have to do too much of the hard work themselves.
- ✧ If the email address of the webmaster isn't obvious from the site, <u>look up the technical contact</u> from the site's domain name record (which you can bring up at sites such as http://whois.sc or http://domainsearch.com).

If you have more time than sense (or business is slow), you might wish to explore the world of reciprocal link building a little further. I include for your delectation a short table of reciprocal exchange sites (itself a summary of a more complete list on my forum). Below are eight of the best known members-only services, ordered by PageRank.

Website	PR	Costs	Notes
www.links-pal.com	6	$2.99 one time	
www.qlew.org	6	Free	Small number of members
www.123exchangelinks.com	5	Free	Over 60,000 members
www.linkexchanged.com	5	$19 per month	
www.linkmarket.net	5	Free	Nearly 80,000 members
www.linkmetro.com	4	Free	Easy-to-use interface
www.links4trade.com	3	$9.95 per month	
www.linkdiy.com	3	$19.95 per month	Approx 7,000 members

I reiterate that you should only exchange links with sites relevant to your own site users. If you find yourself swapping links with casinos, porn sites, and Viagra salespeople, you have probably lost the plot (unless of course that is the business you are in!).

If you are going to build reciprocal links, you need to create an area of your site to hold them. Generally, my advice is to create a Partners page that contains two sections: "featured links" and a small "link directory." The Partners page should be linked from the bottom of your homepage using, if possible, a very innocuous 8-point gray link.

You will use the featured links section of this page to contain no more than 20 links back to sites that require your reciprocal link to be either on a higher PageRank page or from a page that is no more than one click away from your homepage. The link directory section should begin with a short introduction and end with no more than eight links to subpages, each of which contains no more than 25 links. This affords you a maximum of $8 \times 25 + 20 = 420$ links. Note that you should never place more than 25 links on any given page. Try to give your subpages meaningful category titles as well.

Just take my advice though: Reciprocal link building (taken to excess) is a largely fruitless and very time-consuming activity. You are far better off focusing your efforts on some of the other techniques below, to get a smaller number of links from more important sites. If people took half the time they generally spend on reciprocal link requests and reinvested it evenly across all the other areas I am going to tell you about, they would fare ten times better than they generally do.

Directory submission

Web directories are a brave attempt to create a human-maintained taxonomy or classification of the entire web and their numbers have grown dramatically over the last four or five years. By contrast to reciprocal linking, very few search engine marketers would dare suggest that directory submissions are a waste of time. However, it is important to be focused.

I tend to group directories into five categories. One directory may, in fact, fit into more than one category (and most do). Directories may also evolve over time, moving from one category to another. However, the categorization is useful nonetheless:

- ✧ Paid directories, which charge webmasters to list their sites or carry their pay-per-click adverts, either on a one-off basis or using a recurring monthly or annual fee. An example is business.com, one of the oldest and best-established directories on the web.
- ✧ Reciprocal directories, which will list sites but only in exchange for a reciprocal backlink (typically to the homepage of the directory and using keyword-rich anchor text).
- ✧ Free directories, which are prepared to list your site for free (although typically after quite a long wait; people tend to like

doing things for free and there is often a long submission
queue).

✧ Bidding directories, a relatively new type of directory service,
where webmasters bid against each other to maintain key positions in the directory for their chosen keywords.

✧ Deep link directories (whether paid, reciprocal, bidding, or
free), which are prepared to list one or more deep links direct to
the inner pages of your website.

As I have said, many directories fall into more than one category. For
example, some will offer a free submission service (with a long queue),
a free reciprocal service (with a shorter queue), and a paid express-
review service (with a 12–24-hour guaranteed turnaround). You may also
come across the term "niche directory." This describes a directory
focused on a particular industry or interest (for example the UK
Wedding Directory at www.uk-wedding-directory.com). Niche directories are increasingly popular, following Google's increased emphasis on
link relevance, and should definitely be on your shopping list.

The key point about directory services, whatever their type, is that
they are in the business of creating anchor-rich links to sites like yours,
from category pages full of sites relevant to your industry. Some sites are
given much authority by Google, with a PR8 for the Open Directory
Project (www.dmoz.org) and Yahoo! Directory (http://dir.yahoo.com).

Before I consider each directory category more closely, I would like
to outline a few general recommendations for directory submission:

✧ Create both a long (60–70 words) and a short (30–40 words)
description of your site and put them in a text file on your desktop that you can easily copy and paste from. This should be similar to what you came up with for your meta-description tag (see
page 103) and should be sensibly loaded with your best keywords. The longer description is to cater for directories that set
a minimum for the length of the description field.

✧ You may wish to create a number of variants of these descriptions to provide variety and help with future tracking of your submissions.

✧ Create a keyword list of your site-wide keywords and put that in the same text file as your descriptions. Some directories will ask you for a keyword list, so it is good to have this to hand. If the directory you are submitting to does not provide instructions to the contrary, separate each phrase with a comma and no space.

✧ Place a list of your reciprocal link page URLs into the text file. When you do reciprocal directory submissions, you will again need to copy and paste these into input boxes in the directory submission form.

✧ Pay close attention to the style and submission guide for each directory, adjusting your description and link text where necessary. For example, some directories require you to use the name of your business in the link text. If you have chosen a keyword-rich domain, this will make this rule more bearable.

✧ If you do not already have one, create a business PayPal account. Many paid directories use PayPal as their payment method of choice, so you will find it difficult to avoid. Try to load up your PayPal account with your budget in advance, so you can more readily keep a track on what you spend in your campaign.

Paid directories

Paid submissions are often better value than they look and are typically more reliable than any other type of submission. Most of the directories of greatest importance to your rankings are paid only. For this reason, I recommend taking a deep breath before you start and considering your budget.

In a regular offline business, you might happily spend up to $1,500 a year or more for *Yellow Pages* listings. You might cough up a similar sum for a single full-page newspaper advertisement. If your budget runs to radio advertising or cable television, you will be accustomed to laying out even bigger amounts. You might also spend several hundred dollars a month already on paid web advertising.

Why is it, then, that I find so many of my clients reluctant to spend out on directory submissions? After all, most paid submissions are for a one-off fee that then delivers value almost into perpetuity. A newspaper or magazine ad has a shelf life of a month at most. The upside is the very fact that so many people share this reluctance – it gives you an edge. If you are prepared to put aside $4,000 or so for paid listings (and approximately $1,000 per year after that), it may well be the best advertising money you have ever spent.

So set a budget (whatever you can afford) and stick to it. The directory sites listed overleaf are the top 20 best to get started on, as they share high PageRank, established domains, and a respected submission standard, backed by thorough human editing of results. Unless otherwise noted the costs are on a one-time basis.

Of the paid directories Yahoo! is by far the most important (and has a price tag to match). Obtaining a listing in Yahoo! can mean up to 20 different links to your site from the different local instances of the directory around the world. All of these pages have a decent PageRank, so you are getting real value for money. Yahoo! editors are known for their editorial zeal, so you can expect your final listing to differ somewhat from your submission. However, in my experience they are very willing to listen and tweak the listing if you can be persuasive and present a good argument for why they should. Missing out on a Yahoo! listing to save money is a false economy.

Reciprocal directories

The most important factor to look for in reciprocal directories is their reliability. The last thing you want to do is create lots of outbound links from your site that are not quickly and properly reciprocated by the directory owner.

Directory name	Directory URL	Cost	Est.	PageRank
Yahoo!	dir.yahoo.com	$299 p.a.	1995	8
Best of the Web	www.botw.org	$200	1996	7
Business.com	www.business.com	$199 p.a.	1998	7
Clush	www.clush.com/dir	$20 p.a.	2004	7
Elib	www.elib.org	$81	2003	7
Starting Point	www.stpt.com/directory	$99 p.a	1995	7
Alive	www.alivedirectory.com	$50 p.a.	2005	6
Aviva	www.avivadirectory.com	$75 p.a.	2005	6
Chiff	www.chiff.com	$60 p.a.	1998	6
Ezilon	www.ezilon.com	$69	2002	6
Joeant	www.joeant.com	$40	2000	6
Internet Business	www.internetbusiness.co.uk	$30	2004	6
Site Sift	www.site-sift.com	$50	2004	6
UncoverTheNet	www.uncoverthenet.com	$199	2004	6
V7N	directory.v7n.com	$50	2004	6
Abilogic	www.abilogic.com	$18	2003	5
Gimpsy	www.gimpsy.com	$40	2001	5
GoGuides	www.goguides.org	$40	2001	5
Illumirate	www.illumirate.com	$55	2003	5
Qango	www.qango.com	$55	1998	5

The other key area to observe is that many reciprocal directories require you to place the reciprocal link on your site before you can even validate the form submission, let alone get approved for a listing. As some of these reciprocal links carry dynamically generated code (created on the fly when you render the form) you will need to either be in a position to change your links pages in real time or ask someone who can – perhaps your web-design company – to undertake these submissions for you.

Those listed below are, in my experience, the top 20 reciprocal directories; combining reasonable PageRank, fairly well-established domains, and reliability in their response to your submission requests. There are many more listed on the forum (www.seo-expert-services.co.uk).

Directory name	Directory URL	Established	PageRank
Directory Delta	www.directorydelta.com	2005	6
Directory World	www.directoryworld.net	2004	6
Iozoo	www.iozoo.com	2004	6
Link Direc	www.linkdirec.com	2006	5
Sootle	directory.sootle.com	2003	5
T Section Directory	www.tsection.com	2005	5
Post Dotcom	www.postdotcom.com	2006	4
Rise Directory	www.risedirectory.com	2006	4
Sams Directory	www.samsdirectory.com	2006	4
Work At Home	www.wahlinks.com	2005	4
World Directory	www.worlddirectory.in	2005	4
TikiFind	www.tikifind.com	2006	4
I-Searches	www.i-searches.com	2005	3
King of the Web	www.kingoftheweb.net	2004	3
Links To My	www.linkstomy.com	2005	3
Link Directory	www.linkdir.co.uk	2006	3
Premium Sites	www.premiumsites.org	2006	3
URL Chief	www.urlchief.com	2006	3
Webmaster Hole	www.webmasterhole.info	2005	3
Top Dot Directory	www.topdot.org	2006	2

You may wonder why the PageRanks in this table are so much lower than the paid list and the ages younger. There are two reasons for this. First, I have tended to prioritize reliability over ranking in this table, and younger directories tend to be more responsive. Secondly, it is generally true that once reciprocal directories break through into the upper PageRank numbers they tend to turn themselves into fully paid services.

Free directories

It still surprises me just how many directories out there will offer to list your site for free. Some are in the early stages of building their listings, so they are seeking critical mass. Others want to fill the sections of their directories that are more empty. Whatever the reason, it is important to be aware that most free directories are literally inundated with listing requests. Reliability is very important.

While there are, again, many more listed on the forum, those opposite are, in my experience, the most important 15 of the free directories, combining the usual factors of PageRank, age and reliability.

You might just consider paid listings with the free directories (where they are offered). Quite often these are very reasonable (perhaps $1-9 per request) and it could make the difference between an accepted listing and a sometime/never.

Before we leave free directories, I want to take some time to discuss the Open Directory (www.dmoz.org) in a little more detail. No single directory is more loved and loathed by webmasters than this one. DMOZ editorial duties are undertaken entirely by volunteers and each site is reviewed by hand in a process that can (it seems) take many months.

As we have already seen, Google makes use of DMOZ data in some cases to produce SERPs snippets. In times gone by, a listing in DMOZ was enough by itself to deliver a PageRank of at least PR4 and, usually, a decent Google ranking all by itself. However now, for various reasons,

Directory name	Directory URL	Est.	PageRank
Dmoz	www.dmoz.org	1999	8
Librarian's Internet Index	www.lii.org	1998	8
Jayde	www.jayde.com	1996	6
Web World Index	www.webworldindex.com	2001	6
Illumirate	www.illumirate.com	2003	5
Turnpike Directory	www.turnpike.net	1994	5
Web Directory	www.bizdirects.com	2004	4
Mavicanet	www.mavicanet.com	1999	4
Web Searches	www.websearches.info	2004	4
I Mom Links	www.imomlinks.com	2005	3
Little Web Directory	www.littlewebdirectory.com	2005	3
Simple Directory	www.simple-directory.net	2006	3
Sinotribe	www.sinotribe.com	2005	3
Intestyle	www.intestyle.com	2004	2
I Web Info	www.iwebinfo.com	2005	2

getting a DMOZ listing – particularly in categories that are already well served – seems to get more difficult every year. The importance to your Google search position of having a DMOZ listing has also diminished relative to other now equally well-established directories.

I am a great personal supporter of the OpenSource principle at the heart of DMOZ. I would simply counsel you not to get obsessive about a DMOZ listing. Try, try, and try again, but if you don't succeed, know when to quit (with your sanity and free time intact). The following short guide might also help:

✧ Choose the right category. If your business is regionally based, then submit to a specific regional category of DMOZ.

✧ Choose a category that is actively maintained by an editor. You can see if this is the case by looking at the bottom of the listing page.

✧ Start by submitting your site. Then wait three months before sending a polite chasing email to the category editor.

✧ If you hear nothing after a further three months, send an escalation email to the category editor above your category.

✧ If after a further three months you have had no response, ask for assistance in the Open Directory Public Forum and then escalate to DMOZ senior staff.

✧ Do not resubmit your site endlessly, as this clogs up the system and normally sees you pushed back to the bottom of the review queue; nobody likes a spammer. Patience is a virtue here.

Deep link directories

Deep link directories are a very valuable part of your active link-building campaign, in that they offer the opportunity to build links direct to sections, categories, and content pages. They are also important for another reason: It is through building deep links that the aforementioned Holy Grail of indented SERPs results can be achieved (see page 121).

Opposite are my top 15 deep link directories. I have chosen a mixture of high-PR paid services and reciprocal services, for those with both big and smaller budgets.

Sites marked with an asterisk offer five additional deep links as part of the package. Some require a reciprocal link to a page with the PageRank listed. There is a more complete list on my forum.

Do not hesitate to make good use of deep link directories: They are a very powerful way to build up the position of your inner pages and rank well on your longer-tail search terms.

Directory name	Directory URL	Cost	Est.	PR
Excellent Guide	www.excellentguide.com	$49.99 p.a.	2005	7
MozDex	www.mozdex.com	$29.95 p.a.	2004	6
Kwik Goblin	www.kwikgoblin.com	$49.95 o/t	2004	6
Elegant Directory	www.elegantdirectory.com	$39.95 o/t	2005	6
Mingle On*	www.mingleon.com	$29.99 o/t	2004	6
Smittyz	www.smittyzweb.com	$29.95 o/t	2005	6
Your Index	www.2yi.net	$18.95 o/t	2004	6
Links Juice*	www.linksjuice.com	$49.97 o/t	2006	6
Seven Seek*	www.sevenseek.com	$50.00 o/t	2004	6
Links Giving	www.linksgiving.com	$29.00 p.a.	2000	6
Links Arena	www.linksarena.com	$14.00 o/t	2006	6
Goo Linx	www.goolinx.com	Reciprocal	2006	5
Directory Free	www.directory-free.com	PR3 reciprocal	2005	5
LDM Studio	www.directory.ldmstudio.com	PR3 reciprocal	2004	5
Lite Directory	www.litedirectory.com	PR3 reciprocal	2006	5

Brad knows that business cards are by far the most effective of his products for the web (by web searches and KOI). However, business cards are a section on his site, so deep links to this section are crucial. By getting a few inbound links to his homepage and many more to his section page with the anchor text "business cards," he hopes to achieve an indented result pair in the Google top 10.

Search engine submission

Search engine submission is the process of submitting your site URL to the thousands of search engines across the web for them to crawl. SEO firms have traditionally charged for this service and many customers claim to be happy with the results, to my continuing amazement. Other firms have provided automated multiple-submission services, using either online interfaces or desktop software. However, this kind of activity has become greatly devalued in recent years, partly because of the relative dominance of the major engines and also since most decent search engines crawl the web so find websites by themselves quite happily. Nevertheless, search engine results pages for the lesser engines do occasionally get crawled by Google, and for this reason there is a small residual value to search engine submission.

My recommendations, in brief, are as follows:

- ✧ Do *not* use search engine submission software. Many of the programs do not work properly as their links are out of date and some search engines actively block or blacklist such submissions. Google's Guide for Webmasters says: "Don't use unauthorized computer programs to submit pages, check rankings, etc. Such programs consume computing resources and violate our terms of service."
- ✧ To find other search engines, search on Google for the words "submit URL," "submit site," and "add to listing" in turn and work your way slowly through the top 100 results. There are so many search engines, you could well spend a few happy weekends on this activity alone. My advice is to check the PageRank of an engine's homepage before bothering to submit. Anything less than PR4 is not worth the hassle.
- ✧ Use the same description as you used for the directory submissions (where a description is asked for). Always place your homepage URL in the submission box; the engine (if decent) will find and crawl the rest of your pages from there.

I would only bother submitting to the following eight engines (and leave all the rest to people with more time than sense).

Engine name	Engine URL	Notes	Est.	PR
Exactseek	www.exactseek.com	Free, add up to 10 URLs	2000	7
Gigablast	www.gigablast.com	Free	2005	7
EntireWeb	www.entireweb.com	$249 to submit	1998	6
ScrubTheWeb	www.scrubtheweb.com	Reciprocal link to get crawled	1996	6
Ulysseek	www.ulysseek.com	$20 per URL	2005	5
Amfibi	www.amfibi.com	Free/$10 per URL express	2001	0
Search Hippo	www.searchhippo.com	Register first, then free	2001	0
Towersearch	www.towersearch.com	Register first, then free	2002	0

I include entireweb.com and amfibi.com because are the English-language versions of established search engines in Sweden and Spain respectively. I consider two of the big international players, baidu.com and yandex.com, in a brief piece later on within the local search optimization section (see page 210).

Forum participation

Now we get on to one of the most interesting areas of active link building: forum participation. You may have noticed that many posters on forums have beautifully crafted signatures, which show the name of their business (often linked using keyword-rich anchor text). There is a reason for this: Search engines index these links, and in some cases both the forum posts and the profile pages of users – which also carry links – acquire a decent PageRank from Google. On many bulletin boards (for example VBulletin) the syntax for a signature file is as follows:

John Doe, Managing Director
[url=http://www.yourdomain.com]keyword anchor text[/url]

My recommendations for forum participation are as follows:

- ✧ Research areas of interest related to your site through a search on Google. For example, if you are a printer like Brad who serves mainly small businesses, you might search for "small business forum" or "home business forum."
- ✧ Identify no more than three or four forums you can join (selecting from the top 10 results only, where the PageRank of the forum homepage is PR5 or better).
- ✧ Sign up and create a profile page that contains a link to your website or blog, and a signature file containing anchor-rich keywords.
- ✧ Begin posting answers to questions that you are qualified to answer and do not drag up old posts from the archives (forum members will not thank you for this). Remember the etiquette: Be helpful, be polite, and avoid outrageous self-promotion. If you fail to do this, your reputation (and that of your business) could suffer.
- ✧ Try to tie your postings back to advice on your business blog where possible. If, for example, you were answering a question on the merits of full-color printing, you could link back to an article on your blog that examines this in greater detail. In addition to the SEO benefits, you might just acquire a new customer or two. I look at blogging in greater detail in the next section (page 167).
- ✧ Above all, do not go mad with your posts. The value of each link diminishes as the number of them (from the same domain) grows. Remember, you have a business to run!

Articles, newsletters, and ezines

The single best free way to promote your site is article submission. It may not have escaped your notice that there are literally thousands of ezines (electronic magazines) and content sites across the web, covering all manner of specialist subjects. Many of these are run by hobbyists and poorly paid webmasters with very little time on their hands.

In traditional printed media, budding authors and would-be journalists often start their career through getting freelance articles published in newspapers and magazines. An inefficient network of editors and literary agents stand in the way of publication and the pay is poor.

The internet has liberated this market by massively increasing the number of publications seeking material and creating hundreds of online article repositories where anyone can post an article, inviting publication. In addition, there are writing groups and announcement lists where article writers can notify webmasters of their newly written pieces. The way it works is this:

⟡ Create high-quality content (1,000–1,500 words) covering a particular topic or answering a specific question and sharing your hard-earned knowledge and expertise.

⟡ Post your article on up to five high-quality free article repositories, together with a synopsis and a resource box ("about the author") that links back to your website or business blog.

⟡ Signal the presence of your new article by posting it to an announcement list that is monitored by webmasters and ezine editors.

⟡ Webmasters and editors find and "syndicate" your content by adding it to their sites. As you have required them to include the resource box (as a condition for free reproduction), they build excellent backlinks to your site (and send you traffic too).

If you can write good copy, the world of the web is literally your oyster. If you can identify multiple niches where questions lie unanswered, you can (as Matt Cutts puts it) "rock the search engines." The point it that this is what the web should be all about: connecting people who are searching for something to excellent content that answers their questions.

The mathematics are also quite exciting. Imagine you have written ten articles and placed each of them on five article repositories. Each article is picked up by (say) 20 different webmasters each year and republished. That's 10 × 20 × 5 = 1,000 backlinks over five years, with the majority from highly relevant and important sites. That's quite a good return on your modest writing investment.

If you don't believe me, have a look at an article I wrote a few years back about how to name an intranet project. Do an exact-phrase search on Google for "the name one gives a project does have a marked" and click to "repeat the search with omitted results included." At the time of writing 366 sites have syndicated this article since it was written in October 2004. If I had ten articles like this one, I'd have nearly 4,000 backlinks by now.

How to construct your article

When writing articles, planning and preparation are key. I typically create a Word document that contains eight boxes. I use these boxes to copy and paste from when I add the article to the repositories:

- ✧ <u>Box 1: Article title</u>. For my intranet article the title was: Intranet Project Names – Some Ideas.
- ✧ <u>Box 2: Publishing guidelines</u>. The guidelines inform the webmaster what reprint permissions they have, what they cannot modify, and whether they need to seek permission from you or notify you prior to publication. Also included is the permalink URL (a permanent link to your article), author name, contact email, blog address, and article word count.
- ✧ <u>Box 3: Article keywords</u>. Some repositories allow you to specify keyword metadata that will help webmasters find your article. Enter keyword data in this box, separated by a comma but no spaces.
- ✧ <u>Box 4: Article summary</u>. Include in this box a 100–200-word abstract of the content. On many repositories, the title and summary will be what a webmaster looks at first when deciding between your article and others on offer.

- ✧ <u>Boxes 5 and 6: Article body</u>. Include in box 5 a 1,000–1,500-word article written in plain text, with carriage returns both before and after any subtitles. In box 6, produce an HTML version of the same article, with subtitles struck out with heading tags. Do not include more than two anchor-rich links within the body of the article, as many repositories limit the number you can have.
- ✧ <u>Boxes 7 and 8: Resource box</u>. Again, produce plain-text and HTML versions of your resource box, which includes information about the author and an anchor-rich text link back to your website or blog.

Overleaf I have included examples for box 2 (publishing guidelines) and box 7 (resource box).

Where to submit your article

On the forum (www.seo-expert-services.co.uk) I include links to over 100 article repositories. However, my advice is to choose four or five main repositories from the shorter list below. It is better to write more articles than to submit just a few to lots of different places.

Article repository	Notes	Est.	PR
www.articlesfactory.com	Links in body and resource box	2004	7
www.articledashboard.com	Links in body and resource box	2005	6
http://ezinearticles.com	3 links in resource box. HTML	1999	6
www.articleonramp.com	Links in body and resource box	2006	5
www.ideamarketers.com	Link in resource box	1998	5
www.goarticles.com	Preview function. Plain-text body	2000	4

Once you have selected your sites, visit them and sign up for an account. Validate registration as appropriate by email and then set up your articles one by one, choosing the most appropriate category for

Article Title:
Intranet Project Names – Some Ideas

Article URL:
http://viney.com/intranet_watch/2004/10/intranet-project-names-some-ideas.html

Author Name:
David Viney

Contact Email Address:
david@viney.com

Author Blog:
http://viney.com/intranet_watch

Word Count:
1,426 (body)

each. Where sites only support plain-text articles, use boxes 5 and 7 from your template file. Where simple HTML tags are supported, use boxes 6 and 8. If a preview function is available, test your article out prior to submitting it for editorial review and acceptance.

How to announce your article

Once your article has been published, many webmasters will find your article through a regular search. Others may have subscribed to an RSS feed (see page 170) from the repository, so will get notified of your article that way. However, there is another way to let webmasters know: article announcement lists.

All the main article announcement lists live on Yahoo! Groups, as Yahoo! was the first to support decent RSS feed syndication and email feeds from a social networking platform back in 1999. Again, my advice is to choose no more than two or three from the shortlist below.

Article announcement list	Members	Est.	PR
http://groups.yahoo.com/group/article–announce	~10,000	1999	4
http://tech.groups.yahoo.com/group/aabusiness	~6,000	2000	4
http://groups.yahoo.com/group/Free-Reprint-Articles	~4,000	2001	4
http://finance.groups.yahoo.com/group/Free-Content	~4,000	1999	4
http://tech.groups.yahoo.com/group/aainet	~3,000	2000	4

Add your articles (in plain text) to the groups, making sure that you put your publishing guidelines at the top of each post. After checking by the site moderators, the existence of the article will be announced to all members by email. Will your title catch their eye as their email system loads up the 40 or so articles for the day? Perhaps it will and your syndication activities will be up and running.

Permalinking your content

You will have noted from my intranet article example that you had to click on "repeat the search with omitted results included" to see all the backlinked pages. This is due to the operation of the Google duplicate content filter, which I introduced you to in "how Google stores" (page 94). Google is very effective at identifying pages with substantially similar content and transferring duplicate pages into the supplemental index. Don't let this put you off. Hundreds of inbound links (even from supplemental pages) are still useful to your cause.

The most important thing is to ensure that your original article content page (placed on your site or business blog) is not one of the pages consigned to the supplementals. While there is no way to avoid this absolutely, the use of permalinks helps. The permalink (in case you missed it) in the above example was in the resource box:

> View the original article in context at the Intranet Watch Blog (http://viney.com/intranet_watch/2004/10/intranet-project-names-some-ideas.html).

By showing the reader (and Google) where the original source for the article is, you stand a better chance of ensuring that your original content page is the one that stays in the main index. After all, the duplicates (at other sites) will then all carry a link to your original page, while your original page will carry no outbound links to any of the article sites or ezines. This means editing your resource box for every article submitted, but the effort is worth it. On some sites you are able to include more links in the body of the article, and then you can simply place the permalink at the bottom of the article body.

By the way, if these efforts fail and your original ends up in the supplemental index, I recommend revising your original to include some fresh and different text to that submitted to the article sites. Over time, if your original is at least 20% different to the other copies across the web, it should re-enter the main index. Try to vary the text at both the top and bottom of the page body. To test whether you have done enough, put your (revised) URL and the main index copy into the Similar Page Checker Tool at www.webconfs.com/similar-page-checker.php.

Creative Commons licenses

If you have a blog or section of your site where your original articles are collected, it may be worth adding a copyright notice to your page, explaining what rights a visiting webmaster has to copy or reprint your content. Quite often, if a webmaster finds one article of yours that they like, they will visit your site to look for some more. A Creative Commons license is a way to tell them what they can do.

The Creative Commons site (at http://creativecommons.org) provides free tools that let authors easily mark their work with the freedoms they want it to carry. The choices essentially fall into two groups: "all rights reserved" and "some rights reserved." Simply fill out the form and the site generates some HTML (text or button) that you can add to your page footer.

Yahoo! Search offers an advanced search option to look for Creative Commons pages and some webmasters make use of this function to track down content they can reprint. By adding the code you make your articles easier to find.

Brad submits four articles to five different sites in the home business sector. Each article contains one (topical and keyword-rich anchor-text) link to his site in the main body of the article and a link to his site and blog in the resource box ("about the author") at the bottom of the article. All the articles are optimized for his keywords and keyword chains.

He is amazed to find that he gets a lot of direct, high-quality traffic from these sites, that his articles appear near the top of search results on some of his three-word keyword chains, and that this seems to help him acquire PageRank more quickly than any of the other free methods he has used. He is not alone in discovering this – now you too are in possession of this key nugget of information.

Brad manages to get some of his articles accepted for publication in popular small business or home business newsletters. He also creates his own monthly email newsletter that customers can sign up for on his site. This helps him to build a mailing list of high-value customers and create an ongoing relationship with them. He finds, over time, that he gets a lot of repeat business this way, particularly when he peppers his newsletter with regular special offers.

Please do copy Brad. It doesn't take an awful lot of effort to do this and it always pays off more than an endless focus on reciprocal link building.

Online public relations

Online PR is a close cousin of article submission. As with articles, you write a press release, publish it to a PR repository, and hope that other sites will pick it up and use it. Where online PR differs (and is thus arguably more powerful) is that it targets the mainstream news media more precisely. Get it right and your humble release could end up featuring on the website of a major news network. Some PR sites even offer you the opportunity to see your release fed into Google News and Yahoo! News. A single PR7 link from a BBC webpage could be the difference between a top 30 and a top 10 ranking for one of your key search phrases.

Writing a good press release

A useful model for writing good press releases is to answer, in turn, the key questions of why, when, who, and how (I will come to where later):

◇ <u>Why</u> are you writing this release? Essentially, you are after free publicity from well-trafficked sites, an uplift in your search rankings, and keeping your business in the public mind. Simple and aimless self-promotion is never a good reason for a press release.

◇ <u>When</u> should you do a release? Typically, most companies use press releases only when they have something interesting to say. For example, you might have launched a new and innovative product, won an award, or opened a different office. If you can't tie a release to something of genuine interest in your business, wait until a time when you can.

◇ <u>Who</u> are you targeting with this release? Is the intent, for example, to attract business customers or consumers? Are you after a particular kind of person (e.g., male/female, young/old)? The angle from which you write the release must appeal to your target audience and demographic directly or it will not be picked up and used in the right ways.

◇ <u>How</u> are you going to ensure that this release actually gets picked up and used by others? The first and key point here is to make it newsworthy. Remember, the news media are your first "buyers" and are after a story, not an advertisement. Keep the piece short, use a journalistic style, stick to facts that you can support, and be concise.

As an example, suppose you were a wedding limousine business and had recently launched a new "pink limo" service, targeted at same-sex civil ceremonies. Corny, I know, but bear with me. Your press release needs a hook to be newsworthy – an astounding fact, a provocative theme, or a bit of humor go a long way in this. Try researching the market for same-sex weddings and gather key facts on the growth in their popularity. Undertake some market research and interview some of your clients. Get some humorous quotes and some useful anecdotes. Find an angle that would appeal to your target audience.

Let's say that your hook is the controversial view that same-sex couples are more committed right now to life-long partnerships than heterosexual couples are (and that you have backed this with some facts and a bit of humor). The next question is how to link this hook through to your payload (i.e., the new limousine service you are offering).

Perhaps you use the artifice of an interview with yourself, where you talk about how new times demand new services. You could describe the decision to paint the limo pink, the response you have had to it, and where you plan to go next.

A good press release is not a boring advert for your business but a real story of genuine interest to your audience. This is the way to get it picked up by news editors.

How to structure your press release

I mentioned earlier a "journalistic style." In short, this means bringing the most important message of your release (in summary form) through to the top, then repeating it at greater length in the rest of the release. This style has served journalists well for several centuries, so ignore it at your peril. This style also prohibits the use of words like "I," "you," and "we" and the unnecessary use of jargon (without explanation).

The structure of a good press release is almost laid down in stone. Follow these principles very closely or risk your release being ignored on quality grounds alone:

- ✧ Header. As your piece is an online press release, the header should always be "FOR IMMEDIATE RELEASE."
- ✧ Headline. Keep your headline to (ideally) fewer than 20 words, written in bold and with minimal capitalization. It should be catchy and informative at the same time. For example:

  Same-sex partnerships exceed all estimates and drive a whole new generation of wedding services

✧ <u>Dateline and location</u>. Always put this under the headline and often in smaller, gray text (for example 1 June 2008, London).

✧ <u>Body</u>. The body of the press release should always begin with a single, short paragraph that summarizes the whole piece and answers all the questions of who, what, when, where, and why. For example:

> In the first year after civil partnerships became law in December 2005, more than 36,000 people tied the knot; more than the government originally predicted for the first several years! 2006 was indeed the year of the gay wedding, driving huge changes in the wedding industry.

The body continues with the hook, the link, and the payload, where you finally discuss your products and services. Often the link includes one or two quotations from your MD and/or customers. Typically with an online press release the body includes one anchor-rich HTML link to your service (e.g., pink limos) and one link to your website (using your business name as the anchor text).

✧ <u>Boilerplate</u>. What is known as the boilerplate (like the resource box for articles) typically remains unchanged from one release to another and contains a short description of who you are and what you do.

✧ <u>Contact info</u>. Conclude the release with contact details so that a newshound can find out more if they wish. Include contact name, company name, address, phone number, and web address. Where the release concerns more than one company (e.g., a joint venture or takeover), include details of both companies.

Where to submit press releases

First and most importantly, always carry the original of your press release on your own site, preferably in a "news" or "press releases" category under an "about us" section. Secondly, always email your release to the editors of any publications that target your chosen audience.

You should also submit your press release to one or more of the main online PR repositories. There are only really three major players (my top three below), but I have included two more for completeness.

Press release repository	Notes	Est.	PR
www.businesswire.com	Links in body and resource box	1996	8
www.prnewswire.com	Links in body and resource box	1995	8
www.prweb.com	3 links in resource box. HTML	1997	7
www.virtualpressoffice.com	For trade shows and press kits	1996	6
www.prlog.org	Free service. Feeds Google News	1996	4

All the major PR services operate a tiered charging mechanism, where you pay more for additional functionality (e.g., using keyword-rich anchor-text links in the main body) or for greater exposure (e.g., feeding Google News or mailing editors). There are some free services (such as prlog), but generally it is worth paying as long as you genuinely have something interesting to communicate.

4.3 What's new in Web 2.0

Web 2.0 refers to a supposed second generation of internet-based services, such as social networking sites, wikis, lenses, and blogs, which let people collaborate and share information online in ways previously unavailable. If Web 1.0 (the first 15 years of the web) was all about connecting people to information, then Web 2.0 is all about connecting people to people, made possible by the increased penetration of high-speed broadband and wireless networks.

These new platforms are allowing people to communicate peer to peer, whether they're sharing audio or video or reconnecting with colleagues or friends, both old and new. Content is increasingly the job of the site user rather than the site creator, with the role of the latter less editor and more moderator. The top 50 most visited web properties now include sites such as myspace.com, wikipedia.org, youtube.com, blogger.com, craigslist.com, flickr.com, facebook.com, digg.com, and classmates.com. And this kind of networking is not just for personal reasons: sites such as linkedin.com and econsultancy.com allow you to profile your business and communicate with those with the same professional interests.

If the currency of Web 1.0 was relevant, reliable, and rich information, we now need to add the Web 2.0 currency of timely, humorous, and even controversial banter, rumor, and innuendo, often called buzz.

Blogs

One of the best-known features of Web 2.0 is the development of blogs. A blog, short for weblog, is similar to an online journal, containing content and web links, sorted in chronological order, with the most recent at the top. At the time of writing there are over 60 million blogs in the "blogosphere," with thousands being added every day. Andy Warhol's vision that one day everyone will enjoy 15 minutes of fame is coming true before our very eyes.

There is, of course, an awful lot of rubbish on blogs, everything from a spotty teenager's diary to the rantings of your local neo-nazi. However, there is also a lot of very time-critical and highly relevant material. There is no mainstream opinion, editor, or censor to get in the way of aspiring writers or journalists; and indeed, journalists from the mainstream media such as the BBC and Sky have active blogs. The nonprofit Global Voices network (www.globalvoicesonline.org) connects bloggers from every corner of the world and has been responsible for breaking many important stories through an ongoing relationship with the Reuters news network.

Commentary as well as news is benefiting from blogging. Take Andrew Sullivan, who as a homosexual, catholic republican might have struggled to find his full expression through traditional media channels. However his blog, the Daily Dish (http://andrewsullivan. theatlantic.com), is arguably now the most popular political blog on the net (visited by more than 100,000 people a day, about the same as the daily circulation of the *New York Times*).

Many businesses have turned their hand to blogging, with some success. More than 5% of Fortune 500 companies have blogs, from IBM to McDonald's, as do a number of CEOs, most famously Jonathan Schwartz, President and CEO of Sun Microsystems.

From an SEO point of view blogs are also attractive to search engines, as they are frequently refreshed, typically automatically generated in standards-compliant HTML, and contain dense, keyword-rich content that tends to be naturally optimized for search.

Business blogging

If you are going to use a blog in your own business, you need to think seriously about the time commitment it entails. Many would-be bloggers make a start only for their enthusiasm to fall away when the pressures of everyday life get in the way. Aside from this, it is actually quite hard to find something interesting to write about on a regular basis without simply re-hashing yesterday's news or the views of others.

There are a number of different blogging platforms, but one of the providers opposite may be a good place to start.

Blogger is probably the easiest to get started on, while Wordpress is most popular with business bloggers for the wide number of slick templates at your disposal.

Site URL	Comments	Established	PR
www.blogger.com	Free. Powered by Google	1999	8
www.drupal.org	OpenSource. Free	2001	9
www.joomla.org	OpenSource. Free	2005	9
www.movabletype.org	Between $50 and $200	2001	8
www.typepad.com	$14.95 p.m. for full control	2003	8
http://wordpress.com	Free and popular	2000	8

Writing content

My recommendation is to focus on the value you can genuinely add based on your experience. Write about something you know and love. You don't need to post every day – write less often and with greater quality; once a month could well be enough. Tie your blog postings, where appropriate, into your off-page article-writing strategy. A business blog could be the perfect place to hold the original article (and be the permalink for all subsequent syndications of the content).

If you are starting a blog from scratch, why not establish a keyword-rich domain to sit alongside your business site? You can always rehost it on a business site subdirectory later.

Getting noticed

Getting noticed is an eternal issue with blogging, as with any form of self-promotion. Some people are better at it than others, but the answer depends on the nature of your blog. If, like Brad, you plan to publish content for small businesspeople on the merits of different types of printing, then you must accept that this is unlikely to become part of the mainstream consciousness. If, however, you plan to be at the cutting edge of a political or social debate (or to be seen as an expert on a topic of wider interest), then you could hope for more.

For the specialist like Brad, I recommend limiting your ambitions to a permalink home for your article posts. If you are more mainstream, then make some effort to comment on the blogs of writers in your field with which you fundamentally agree or disagree. Exchange respect, then exchange links and trackbacks. More will follow.

Either way, you should submit your blog to some of the leading blog directories, the most important of which is Technorati (www.technorati.com). Below is a shortlist to get you going; further resources, as usual, are available on the forum.

Site URL	Requirements	Established	PR
www.technorati.com	Registration & claim code	2002	8
www.blogcatalog.com	Reciprocal button	2004	7
www.bloghub.com	Registration	2003	7
www.blogflux.com	Registration	2005	7
www.britblog.com	No reciprocal	2004	6
www.blogtoplist.com	Two reciprocals	2004	6
www.blogdirs.com	Reciprocal link	2005	5

Getting syndicated

To get people to syndicate or subscribe to your blog there is really only one game in town. Really Simple Syndication (RSS) is a lightweight XML format designed for sharing headlines and other web content, such as product and special-offer information – sort of an automatically distributable "What's New" for a site or a blog.

RSS feeds are readily indexed by search engines and, more importantly, provide a useful stream of user traffic; many users now use online or desktop-based newsreaders, or even their browser, to pull together different feeds they are interested in. In a sense, people are now making their own newspapers, with RSS feeds as the automated publisher-in-chief. Whenever users click on a headline, they are returned to the linked page on the originating site. Every major blogging platform provides out-of-the box RSS feed generation, and a user interested in your content just pushes the button at the bottom of your blog and specifies which reader they want to use.

Getting your new RSS feed found by the search engines is also now simple to do. Sign up for Google Reader, MyYahoo!, and MyMSN respectively, then add your feed to their services. Spidering normally takes no more than 24–48 hours.

The most effective way to get your RSS feed indexed elsewhere is to ping your feed to the main providers by visiting the magical resource Ping-O-Matic (at http://pingomatic.com). Enter your blog title, blog URL, and RSS feed location (usually your blog URL plus /rss.xml, but you can confirm that in your blog settings). Ping-O-Matic does the rest, getting you indexed at multiple sites including Feed Burner, Feedster, Syndic8, NewsGator, PubSub.com, Moreover, Icerocket, and Technorati.

Making it easy to syndicate your feed

There are essentially five ways to help other webmasters syndicate your content. These vary from extremely simple to fairly complex. Unfortunately, the most complicated way (the last) is the most effective.

✧ Browser syndication. Many users simply use the auto-detect capabilities of their browser (i.e., Firefox Live Bookmarks and Internet Explorer 7.0) to spot feeds, then click in the menu bar to make an RSS bookmark. To help people do this, add <link rel="alternate" type="application/rss+xml" title="Jon Doe's Blog Feed" href="http://doe.com/feed.xml" /> to the <head> tags of all the pages on your site.

✧ Feed reader syndication. Recent statistics from FeedBurner suggest that the top five feed readers (Google Reader, MyYahoo!, Bloglines, Netvibes, and Newsgator) account for more than 95% of all views and clicks. However, rather than add a subscribe button for each to every post, why not simply get a subscribe button from www.addthis.com and personalize it for the readers you prefer.

✧ Email subscription. While it sounds somewhat retro, subscription by email is actually quite a recent introduction to the market. Most of us visit our email first during a typical computer session. Many like the convenience of having posts from their favorite blog sent direct to their email inbox. Visit www.feedburner.com to create a button for your site to do this.

✧ Javascript syndication. All of the above methods help a user to read your feed, but if they are going to display that feed on their own website, they need some code. A hosted service is available at FeedSweep (www.feedsweep.com) that will build the code for you. Then put the code in a little box on the sidebar of your blog, so that webmasters can copy and paste from it.

✧ PHP syndication. Search engines do not always love content-rich RSS feeds; or rather, they do not love them if they are wrapped in the programming language Javascript (as is the case with 95% of all syndicated feeds on the web). Google will not read them. If you offer webmasters a PHP syndication code snippet, by contrast, then all your anchor-rich feed links will appear in the HTML of the syndicating site. While this isn't for the total novice, PHP script inclusion is really not so very difficult. Others can help more with this on my forum, but the service I recommend is CARP-KOI evolution (see www.geckotribe.com).

Tagging

A new term has been coined recently, WILF, standing for "what (was) I looking for?" This describes the instantly recognizable phenomenon of the internet user who has forgotten by the end of their session what they had originally set out to do. The Web 2.0 answers to this problem are portable bookmarking (e.g., Google Bookmarks) and social tagging (e.g., del.icio.us), allowing users to maintain and categorize lists of the pages and sites they like most and to remember them for the future. In essence, this is a new voting system to challenge the current proxy of relevance used by search engines, inbound links.

Google and Yahoo! have already taken steps toward personalized search results, where once you're logged in, the search engine remembers sites you have visited more often and positions those sites higher in your future search results. Google has also started experimenting with swickis, custom search engines you can build yourself, covering niche areas (take a look at www.google.com/coop/cse). For example, one might build a Google-powered family saloon car search engine and invite others to use it. Eurekster.com takes a community-based approach to search, and rollyo.com (powered by Yahoo!) allows you to "roll your own" search of up to 25 sites. Search rolls can be shared with other users, added to your site, and more.

There are now a large number of social bookmarking and tagging services, most of which permit members to share their tags with other users and the public at large. In addition, you can subscribe to other people's tags. According to eBizMBA, the 10 largest social bookmarking services (as at October 2007) are as follows:

1 digg.com	2 Technorati.com
3 del.icio.us	4 Propeller.com
5 StumbleUpon.com	6 reddit.com
7 Fark.com	8 MyBlogLog.com
9 Slashdot.org	10 kaboodle.com

On most services a user's public list appears on a web page – a web page that will get crawled by the search engines. As each tag on the user page is rendered as an outbound link, those links carry weight in the traditional, link-based algorithm. Where user pages are subscribed to, those subscriptions get rendered as links too (on the user page of the person making the subscription). In this way, the most popular user lists begin to attract a relevance ranking in their own right.

So it is clear that inbound tags must be seen in the same light as inbound links. The smart webmaster will make it easy for internet users to tag or bookmark their pages, and will ensure that their content includes controversial, topical, newsworthy, or funny material that is likely to attract many tags from surfers.

Getting others to tag your content

In order to bait a link or a tag (just as you do with getting people to pick up your PR stories), you need a hook. Hooks come in a variety of flavors and some of the more popular include:

- ✧ Resource hook. Examples include a plug-in for bloggers, a list of key industry resources, a set of definitions of key technical terms in the industry, a news feed, or a blog on changes in the industry.
- ✧ News hook. Write the definitive review or analysis of a breaking change or development in your industry. Add a long list of references and links to make it even more valuable.
- ✧ Attitude hook. Have a controversial take on an industry issue that runs counter to or in direct conflict with other leading experts. People love a good argument!
- ✧ Humor hook. Present a humorous take on the challenges in your industry, for example 10 popular mistakes when..., famous disaster stories in..., or you know you're an x when you...

Making it easy to tag your pages

In addition to getting people to visit your site, it is vital to make it easy for them to tag your content. For example, you may have noticed blog pages that have 20 or more buttons on them, for a number of social tagging services as well as feed readers. While many blogging engines can partially automate the code of each button to make it correct and unique for each page, you might think that doing this manually for each of your regular web pages seems like a lot of work. You would be right!

FORUM TOOLS However, there is an alternative: tag button aggregators. Via the forum (www.seo-expert-services.co.uk) you can find an up-to-date list of the key players. For the purposes of this chapter I will look at the most popular of these at time of writing, www.addthis.com, which you may remember from the discussion on syndication (page 172).

You can copy and paste some code onto your pages that displays a single AddThis button. When a user clicks on this simple but clever Javascript button, they are taken to a dynamically generated page on the AddThis servers, which offers them a full list of all the tagging services popular enough with users to merit an appearance.

This has three main advantages for you:

✧ You do not need to work out the tag code for any of your pages, AddThis does this automatically.
✧ You only need to have one button, not many, saving you lots of space on the page.
✧ As and when new tagging services emerge and others die out, you do not have to keep on monitoring the situation and rewriting your pages; AddThis does that for you.

As the brand recognition of AddThis and other aggregators improves, so will the propensity of users to click on the button. If you make it easier for them to tag your pages, there is a greater chance of them doing so.

Wikis

A wiki is a website that is written by its users. Visitors can edit and expand its content and wikis tend to operate as communities. The most famous and most important of these sites is <u>Wikipedia</u>, a multilingual, free-content encyclopedia project.

At the time of writing Wikipedia has more than 9 million articles in more than 250 languages, over 2 million of which are in English. Needless to say, this makes it the world's largest, most extensive, and fastest- growing encyclopedia. All the 75,000 contributors are volunteers and any page can be edited by anyone with access to the web. Remarkably, the reputation of the site for quality and reliability (despite numerous challenges) continues to grow.

Google loves Wikipedia. There is no other way to put it. Try a little experiment yourself: Search for your top 10 favorite celebrities one after another on Google. I am prepared to bet that not a single one will have their Wikipedia entry outside the top 10. In fact, try just about any information-based search and Wikipedia will be right up there. It doesn't stop there – look at the PageRank of the pages themselves.

The prominence of Wikipedia in Google SERPs has led many webmasters to try to plant links back to their site somewhere on a relevant Wikipedia page. So if you can write an authoritative article on a suitable topic – or improve on one already there – then do so. Incorporate some of your own original content into the wiki and then link out to a (hopefully more complete) analysis on your site from the references section of the article. Aside from giving you an inbound link with a high PageRank, this will also bring you substantial traffic.

This is not unethical. I am assuming that your content – and your link – will be of genuine value rather than spam. Even if it were spam, I am confident that the ever vigilant Wikipedia community would remove your link before Google had even had the chance to spot it.

A topic is worthy for inclusion in Wikipedia only if it is notable. A topic is presumed to be notable if it has received significant coverage in reliable independent sources. So there is little point in creating a new wiki stub for yourself or your business if neither meets that test. The page you spent hours crafting will be pulled down in less than a week.

There are other wiki sites that may be worth a visit as well, but again if you add content it is important that it is relevant and appropriate:

- ✧ www.citizendium.com (a split from Wikipedia)
- ✧ www.webopedia.com (free internet information)
- ✧ www.aboutus.org (where you can legitimately add content about your company)
- ✧ www.bbc.co.uk/dna/h2g2/ (hosted by the BBC)

Lenses

Founded by notable blogger and marketing guru Seth Godin in 2006, Squidoo is a platform for lenses: single pages, set up by anyone for free, on a topic they know well or care a lot about. Squidoo has grown strongly and is now one of the top 500 internet properties in the world.

On Squidoo, experts and hobbyists build a page about their passions, linking to Flickr photos, Google Maps, eBay auctions, Amazon wishlists, and YouTube videos (to name but a few). Lensmasters can monetize their creations and also share the spoils with charity.

Why not check out if there is a search term related to your business that has not yet been claimed? If there is, sign up and create your first lens. Fill the page, ethically, with useful information for the reader – then link through to more on your site.

4.4 Avoiding penalties

Over the course of this book so far, I have introduced you to the legitimate, ethical, and "white hat" SEO techniques at your disposal. It is time now to briefly consider the world of "black hat" SEO – or, to put it another way, scamming the search engines. Most of its weapons relate to illegitimate link-building tactics.

As Yoda said in *The Phantom Menace*, "Fear is the path to the dark side; fear leads to anger, anger leads to hate and hate leads to suffering." So it is with SEO. The beginning of the journey to the dark side lies in fear: your own fear that your site and its content will not be good enough, on their own, to secure a decent rank. Next is anger at your less than worthy competitors who seem to do far better than you. This leads to hate: hatred of Google and all its minions, and a determination to crush it using means fair or foul. But the suffering comes when your site is banned (or significantly deflated) as a penalty for your misdemeanors.

Google's stated aim of "do no evil" must be your maxim too. Like Luke Skywalker, you must do battle with the forces of darkness, armed only with the living force. Ok, enough! Back to reality. What I am saying is that there are some unscrupulous search engine optimization and promotion techniques that I did not cover in the earlier sections. However, I need to show you just enough of what the dark side is so that you know what to avoid – and so that you can rat on your competitors to Google when you see them misbehaving.

Search engine ethics

Borrowing from the Wild West rather than *Star Wars*, white hat SEO generally refers to ethical techniques, black hat to the unethical ones. Black hat practitioners tend to see search engine optimization as a war and search engines as the enemy. White hatters tend to view search engines as friends who can help them get business.

Search engines are designed to help people find genuinely relevant results for the search terms they enter, in a ranked order. Relevancy is a mixture of the "authority" of the site generally and the specific relevance of the page content to the search made. Anything that undermines this (e.g., by creating a false impression of authority or relevance) is unethical because it undermines the key purpose of the search engine.

Google usefully outlines (and periodically revises) its definition of unethical SEO through the Google Webmaster Guidelines (see the topmost link on www.google.com/support/webmasters). I will take you briefly through the most important points below.

Hidden page text

Some black hatters create hidden text in page code (not intended for humans), often using external style sheets (i.e., outside the document itself). At a simple level, this could be white text on a white background. The text is generally hidden because it does not fit with the rest of the page content but does help with search engine results. This by definition means that as a human searcher, you are likely to be disappointed by the result when you land on this page.

One advanced technique is to use CSS (cascading style sheets) or Javascript positioning or layering to roll hidden text under actual page copy. It may well be the case that Google is unable to readily detect all of these techniques and black hatters thrive at the technical boundaries of what a spider can spot.

Google's Webmaster Guidelines implore you to "make pages for users, not for search engines. Don't deceive your users, or present different content to search engines than you display to users." The guide goes on specifically to recommend that you "avoid hidden text or hidden links." If you want to avoid being blacklisted by Google, pay attention to this advice.

Buying inbound links

Google also requests you to

> avoid tricks intended to improve search engine rankings. A
> good rule of thumb is whether you'd feel comfortable explain-
> ing what you've done to a website that competes with you.
> Another useful test is to ask, "Does this help my users? Would
> I do this if search engines didn't exist?"

The Webmaster Guidelines specifically state: "Don't participate in link
schemes designed to increase your site's ranking or PageRank."

You can find links from PR8 sites on sale for $200. From our ear-
lier exploration of PageRank, you'll understand why such a high price
can be supported. But as you can imagine, Google and others frown on
this activity, as it undermines the whole principle of democracy on
which PageRank is founded.

However, there are two problems for Google in combating the purchase of text links. The first, interestingly, is an ethical one: Google itself
is in the business of selling links, through Google Adwords, and this is
where the vast majority of its revenue and profits come from. At what
point does protecting digital democracy become stifling possible competitors? There are interesting antitrust issues wrapped up in that question; an issue that surely cannot be lost on Google. I also believe, as do
many, that some Google Adwords links do get indexed by Google from
time to time (particularly in the search results of sites like Lycos). As
such, Google's own paid links can have a positive impact on the organic
position of its pay-per-click customers. Would Google ban itself?

Secondly, and perhaps more importantly, many sponsored links are
designed not for search engines but for traffic acquisition. A prominent
link on an industry ezine, for example, could be of great benefit to the
paying website in terms of the referrals that flow from clicks. How does
one algorithmically distinguish between valid paid links (for traffic

acquisition purposes) and those designed to inflate organic rankings artificially? I wouldn't want to have to program that fuzzy logic!

To date Google has favored use of the "report paid links" form (accessible from Google's Webmaster console). On this form one can enter the website selling links, the website buying links, and any additional details to support the case. There are nevertheless two key problems with this snitching method. First, a huge human effort would be required to police the entire web and submissions via this form. Secondly, there is the question of whether Google would actually be prepared to take action against larger websites. Many sites selling links, for example, include genuine educational establishments seeking to raise a little extra cash. If a major US university were to be banned from the rankings, could that university take legal action against Google?

So where does this leave us? The facts are as follows:

✧ Buying links is ethically wrong in a digital democracy and the practice is, in principle, prohibited by Google.
✧ Many text-link brokers still exist, do good business, and have high PageRank homepages (despite the fact that they have been notified to Google many times).
✧ Link broker sites themselves would argue that they are competitors to Google and are only seeking to pursue the same business model that has so benefited Google. On many levels, it is difficult to dispute this.
✧ Sites do buy links and get away with it. The positive effect on rankings can be substantial, particularly for those with deep pockets.

I would advise you to avoid this sort of activity altogether, as I do not think that buying links is worth the risk. Your competitors may well notify Google of your activity and there is always the possibility that Google will take action. However, as I have said, some do get away with it – so, if you like a gamble, you can indulge your risk appetite at the places overleaf.

Site URL	Comments	Est.	PR
www.textlinkbrokers.com	Protects the identity of sites	2003	6
www.linkadage.com	Only provides thumbnail	2003	6
http://automatedlinkexchange.com	Link placement network		

Certain types of legitimate paid links are ethical and I am not discouraging them. The most common of these include:

- ❖ A prominent link on content-rich sites (including online newspapers and ezines) designed solely to acquire traffic.
- ❖ Donations made to political parties, OpenSource software sites, and other voluntary organizations (where the donor is credited on a donations page with a backlink).

I will leave you wandering in that moral maze and move on to areas of more clear-cut abuse.

FFAs and IBLNs

Or free-for-all link farms and independent backlinking networks, to expand the acronyms. In its Webmaster Guidelines, Google says:

Don't participate in link schemes designed to increase your site's ranking or PageRank. In particular, avoid links to web spammers or "bad neighborhoods" on the web as your own ranking may be affected adversely by those links.

In practice, Google identifies "bad neighborhoods" by devaluing backlinks from the same IP subnet. Where a site is simply a link farm site (which lists loads of links to other sites, in exchange for links back or money), Google will eventually identify it as a bad neighborhood and deflate the value of the links in its index.

IBLNs are networks of sites that all directly or indirectly link back to your site in such as a way as to promote it through the search engine rankings. The way IBLNs get around Google's IP monitoring is by using a completely different web-hosting plan for every site you want to link back directly to you.

This is very time consuming and will cost you a lot of money. It is also not foolproof and if detected, can lead to Google simply wiping from its index all the direct referrers (the sites it finds built simply to link to your main site) or, worse, dropping your entire IBLN, including the main site you were trying to optimize for. Don't be daft – keep it clean!

Cloaking pages or sneaky redirects

Google recommends that you "avoid 'doorway' pages created just for search engines, or other 'cookie cutter' approaches such as affiliate programs with little or no original content."

Cloaking is a technique where search engines are served different content to what a human user sees (for example delivering a text page to search engine spiders and a flash page to users). Webmasters achieve this by either detecting the user agent that is visiting the site and redirecting it to a different page if it appears to be a spider; or using redirects placed in Javascript, which robots don't follow but browsers do, to redirect human users to a different page.

Doorway pages are those made specifically for search engines and normally contain hundreds of links designed to pass PageRank rather than entertain the user. Google insists that where links pages are used, they are split up into manageable sections. Many have seen this as an indicator that Google differentiates between real and doorway pages simply by counting the number of outbound links on the page. I tend to agree (hence my earlier advice to organize any reciprocal link directory into categories and to limit the number of links on a page). Now you know why: I want you to avoid stumbling into a trap that wasn't designed for you.

Dealing with Google penalties

Well, my young apprentice (as Yoda would say), you are now knowledge-able in the ways of the dark side. Avoid black hat techniques at all costs, even when you see your competitors getting away with them. Report others if you can and continue along a harder, but ultimately more rewarding path.

Most importantly, check at all times that you are not inadvertently doing something on your site for legitimate, ethical reasons that might trigger a spam penalty from Google.

To check for mistakes in the coding of your site that could put you at risk, pay a visit to the Search Engine Spam Detector at http://tool.motoricerca.info/spam-detector. Using this tool, you can put in the URL of each of your pages in turn and look for instances of what might seem suspicious behavior to a spam-detecting algorithm. Normally, many of these items are easy to correct without affecting the visual impact or usability of your site significantly.

If it all goes wrong and your site does indeed appear to have been banned by Google, then it's probably time to seek some professional help. Indicators of a ban include a massive drop in Google-recorded backlinks; far fewer visits to your site from Googlebot; and even, on rare occasions, a message from Google in your webmaster console! Before you do seek help, try to correct any of the issues in your code that may be hurting you; revise and rename your sitemap; and request reinclusion via the link in Webmaster Tools.

Step 5: Paying for position

Rather than paying for links, there are of course more direct ways of paying for an improved search engine position.

Run a search on Yahoo! or Google for a popular consumer product like MP3 players. In the results you'll see a set labeled as sponsored links or sponsored results. Some results appear in colored text boxes along the site of the page, while others may appear in the same format as the main search results. All these results are paid advertisements from the sites listed within the ads, known as <u>pay per click</u> or PPC.

The ranking order of an ad on Google is based on the product of three factors: the amount bid by the advertiser, the popularity of the ad, and the quality of the landing page to which the ad leads. Advertisements are purchased through the Google Adwords program, either directly or via paid marketing agencies. Google's Adwords are displayed on Google, AOL, and Ask Jeeves, while another large program, Yahoo's Sponsored Links, appears on Yahoo!, MSN, AltaVista, and others. MSN has also opened its own AdCenter service, which currently runs a poor third to the other two.

If you have tried and failed with regular organic campaigns, the chances are that you are operating in a highly competitive arena where a PPC campaign may well be justified. However, I would argue that most paid advertising is already too expensive and will become even more so. You need to think seriously about where paid search fits in your strategy. The fact is that only about 35% of searchers ever click on paid results and most web users consider organic results to be more authoritative (as they have been earned by reputation rather than bid for with money). **So the right way to view paid advertising is as a useful adjunct to a decent organic campaign, rather than the other way around.**

You will remember my previous analogy of SEO being like shooting at targets with a limited number of bullets. In organic campaigns, you are limited by your time, the tolerance of your customers, the number of pages your website can support, and the Google spam filters. In a paid campaign, there are no such limits.

You will also remember my assertion that organic SEO can take up to 18 months to have an effect due to age-deflation factors in the Google algorithm. Paid results, by contrast, take effect immediately and start a stream of traffic to your site.

This brings me to what I see as the six valid uses for paid advertising within a well-managed overall campaign:

◇ Testing how well certain keyphrase combinations work during the planning phase of an organic campaign (i.e., before you commit serious resources to their organic optimization).

◇ Temporary boosting of traffic levels during the period before an organic campaign has taken full effect in the search engine results.

◇ Permanent use in the targeting of long-tail phrases (where constraints on your website, in particular, make organic lines of attack less attractive).

◇ Permanent use in very competitive main search terms where organic dominance may take years to achieve.

◇ Permanent use in short-lived business promotional campaigns and sponsorship deals (real advertising!) where a permanent web presence is not necessary.

◇ Permanent use in the qualification of leads, through the use of advanced match drivers not possible with organic search results.

The first two points are self-explanatory and the other four will be covered during the rest of this chapter. Before we look more closely at the methodology and strategies for paid marketing, I first walk you through the stages of a first-time Google Adwords set-up (explained further at http://adwords.google.com/select/Login).

Setting up Google Adwords

First, create a Google account in order to be able to track your return on investment more easily later. Visit https://www.google.com/ accounts/NewAccount and put in an email address, password, and location. Agree to the terms and complete the CAPTCHA challenge. Once you have verified your submission by returning the email you are sent, you can log in to your account.

Now create a Google Adwords account. Visit https://adwords. google.com and click on the "Start" button, then the "Create account" button and the "Standard edition." Your first step will be to <u>select your target customers</u> by language and location.

My first piece of advice is to be honest with yourself. How many punters are likely to come from all those countries on the list? Can you support interaction with customers whose first language isn't English? At least to begin with, stick to serving ads only in your main country and language of operation. If you are based in the US, you might consider adding Canada, but not specifying French as a language unless you're fluent.

Note that specifying a tighter region for your ads will result in fewer ads being served, but should increase your conversion rate. For example, if Brad specified "Idaho" or simply "Boise ID" (both of which are options) he will get less traffic – mainly from users in the Boise area – but probably sell more stuff from the traffic he gets.

There are three further points to note with regional selections. First, if you select specific regions your ads will not be served on the AOL network. Secondly, your ads will appear alongside location-specific searches regardless of the user's location. For example, if someone in Venezuela searched on "printers Boise Idaho," Brad's ads would be served. Thirdly, you cannot set up region-specific searches for multiple different regions without setting up more than one Adwords account.

Choose your regional matches and you are ready to <u>set up your first ad</u>. I cover optimizing your ads later in this chapter; for now, I want to outline briefly the different parts of the ad:

✧ Headline (max 25 characters). The headline will ultimately appear underlined and in blue within the sponsored search listings and will be linked to your destination URL (see below).

✧ Description (max 70 characters). Split over two lines of 35 characters each, the description is an advertising strapline that sits under the headline. Each line is truncated to complete words, so in practice you may have fewer than 70 characters to work with.

✧ Display URL (max 35 characters). This is the URL of your site and is usually done in the format http://www.yourdomain.com. It simply reminds the searcher which business the ad comes from.

✧ Destination URL (max 1,024 characters). This points to the landing page for this particular ad and defines where the user will be taken to after clicking on the headline anchor text.

The key to writing effective Google ads is to remember that you have to grab the interest of the reader in a very few characters. When we turn to methodology we cover the tips and tricks in some detail. For now, merely create a simple ad that points to your homepage and move on to choosing your keywords.

While Google suggests some keywords for you based on the on-page elements of your site, the best way to load your keywords is to type each of your main keyword categories, one by one, into the search box. Try, like Brad, "business cards" and fully expand the results; you may be surprised how many there are. Add just one of your own keywords to your basket at this point as you are going to do the hard work later. Ignore too, for now, the advanced option of match types and move on to the next screen, setting pricing.

Here you set up the currency with which you'd like to pay, your daily budget, and your default bid for the cost per click (CPC). For now, set your budget to $1 per day and your default bid to the absolute minimum (currently $0.01). In practice you will have to increase your bids and your budget over time, but it is better to start low and build rather than the other way around. I know of many people who have burnt their way through thousands of dollars in just a few days before really knowing what they were doing. Don't make the same mistake!

The final step in the sign-up process is to enter an email address and verify that by email. Log in to your account and enter your payment information. I recommend to clients that they contract on a pre-paid basis, as this provides an extra level of budgetary control. Accept the terms and conditions, then enter your credit card information and billing address. Note that you will be charged a $5 fee for account activation and then will need to pre-pay a minimum of $10 to get started.

Now you've signed up, you can turn your attention to the individual parts of this step of your SEO campaign.

5.1 Match driver selection

Match drivers are basically the paid search equivalent of keywords. However, paid search offers a level of qualification not possible in organic SEO. You can, as we have already seen, choose the location and language in which you want ads to appear. Through day parting, you can select the times of day at which you wish your ads to be served. More importantly, you can not only select the positive phrases on which you wish ads to be served, but also exclude searches that include negative qualifiers.

To set up your first campaign, log in to your Adwords account and visit the campaign summary category of the campaign management tab. You will see "campaign #1" in the online campaigns table. Each campaign holds a number of ad groups and each ad group consists of a number of ads. Campaign #1 contains the ad you set up when you registered (within ad group #1).

Edit the campaign to give it a more meaningful name. For example, Brad renames his campaign "Business Cards." At this point you can specify at what times of the day you would like the ad to appear. Think about your customers. Are they only likely (during the working week) to buy (rather than browse) at lunch or in the evening? If so, why not day part your ads for Monday–Friday to serve only during those times?

For now, choose the options "show ads evenly over time," "enable position preferences," and "display better-performing ads more often." We will return to these later under bid and campaign management.

Next, rename your ad group #1 to something more meaningful. Brad is going to have three main ad groups within the Business Cards campaign: Luxury Business Cards, Cheap Business Cards, and Short Run Business Cards.

Positive keyword matching

Go back to your first ad group, where you should see the single-keyword phrase you set up earlier. Select the "edit keywords" option to bring up the Keyword and CPC edit dialogue. You will note that there are three types of positive match option available to you:

- ✦ Broad match. This is the most flexible of the match options, as Google automatically runs your ads on all variations of your keywords, even if those terms are not precisely in your keyword list. Google likes broad match and sets it as the default, because it can serve more ads for you and therefore make more money. You will not be using it if you are wise, because although you maximize the number of click-throughs, you lose control over the qualification of customers; more on this below.
- ✦ Exact match. If you surround your keywords with square brackets (e.g., [luxury business cards]) your ad will only appear when someone types that exact search query. For example, the ad would not be served to someone querying "luxury business cards online." This tends to maximize conversion rates, as you only receive customers looking for exactly what you have to offer. However, it results in a large decrease in the number of click-throughs. For this reason, exact match is also not the best option to use.

✧ <u>Phrase match</u>. If you surround your keyword with quotation marks (e.g., "luxury business cards"), your ad will appear whenever someone enters a search query that contains that exact phrase, even if they place other words before or after it. For example, a search for "luxury business cards online" and "print your own luxury business cards" would still serve an ad phrase matched on "luxury business cards." This is the right option to use in most cases.

Phrase match should be your choice. For now, simply add quotation marks around your first search phrase and move on. We will come back to more advanced use of this dialogue box later.

Negative keyword matching

Negative keyword matching is perhaps the most powerful of all Google Adwords features and is in itself an excellent reason for using paid marketing. It allows you to avoid serving ads to anyone who has included a particular trigger word in their search query, irrespective of whether the rest of the query is a good match.

Let's consider an example. Mary Phillips sells luxury handbags by mail from her online business based in Sacramento, California. You know the sort of thing: Louis Vuitton, Fendi, and Gucci are her most popular ranges. She has been going broke on Adwords paying for broad-match phrases like "buy handbags online," but finding that many of her customers never complete a purchase. After investigating her web logs, she realizes that many searchers look for "cheap handbags," "handbags sale," and the like; exactly the wrong sort of searches for luxury handbag sales.

After reading this book, Mary switches to phrase-match terms and sets a negative keyword matching list that includes the following terms:

> free, budget, cheap, discount, sale, "cut rate," "marked down,"
> inexpensive, affordable, "low priced," reduced, reasonable, factory,
> warehouse

Following this her number of click-throughs falls by more than 60% but
her number of sales stays exactly the same. This allows Mary to increase
the range of terms she targets and to bid separately on exact-match
terms like "luxury handbags" and more.

The best place to set negative keyword matching is at the campaign
summary level, so return there. Click on the "Add" link to bring up the
"edit campaign negative keywords" dialogue. Add your own negative
matches one by one.

5.2 Ad text optimization

Welcome to the biggest challenge in copywriting: How do you compel a
user to click on a link when all you have to work with is 25 characters
for the title, 70 for the ad itself, and 35 characters for the URL?

Your goal has to be to create a title and text that are so captivating
that the reader very quickly feels that they must know more about this
subject or service. Because your ad will be shown to people who have
already expressed an interest in knowing about the subject of your website, you want to convince them that yours is the only place to learn or
buy what they want.

Optimizing title and text

You will remember, no doubt, my evaluation of the "call to action" in
the section on SERPs snippets (page 118). In your Google ad this
becomes all the more important. Verb–noun, action-oriented constructs
that instantly sell the benefits work best. For example, ad titles like "lose
weight" and "stay looking younger" tend to convert better than their

duller counterparts "dietary advice" and "sun block cream." Similarly, qualifying words like "free," "new," and "sale" typically attract a user's attention as their benefits tend to speak for themselves.

If the purpose of the link headline is to grab attention, the descriptive phrase serves both to dispel doubt and to qualify the click-through, encouraging emotion and commitment on the part of the right customers and avoidance on the part of the wrong ones. Typically, this involves both a feature and a (qualified) benefit. Compare these two ads:

High Quality Mutual Fund
Top performing fund in last 5 years
Rewards those saving for retirement

High Quality Mutual Fund
Fund designed for the self-employed
Top performance & flexible payments

I think you can see right away that very different people are likely to click on each ad. The first appeals to the older, less risk-loving, future retiree. The latter appeals to someone younger, who perhaps values flexibility in making payments over anything else. Both ads, however, establish that the fund is a top performer (the benefit) and hint at features (i.e., that the fund is designed for a particular niche).

There are one or two more things to notice about this ad. First, the words "mutual fund" are used in the title and repeated (albeit just as "fund") in the description. This is all about quality scores (as the main search phrase category being targeted is "mutual fund"). Secondly, the use of terms like "high quality" and specific claims like "top performance" are normally frowned on by Google; to survive editorial review, your landing page must clearly back up this claim with independent and verifiable evidence, or your ad will be rejected.

You want a high click-through rate (CTR) from your ads. However, you also want high conversion of those click-throughs to goal completion on your site (e.g., "download fund prospectus" or "book a financial consultation"). If you are a fund specializing in investments for the self-employed, anyone other than the self-employed is likely to click through but then leave your site in a hurry. This may seem fairly obvious to you, but it is amazing how many businesses make the fundamental mistake of chasing click-throughs without also considering conversion. This is the easiest way to lose money known to humanity!

Split testing

Always test two (or more) ads simultaneously; in traditional print advertising this is what is known as an A/B split test. Generally, you run both ads together to find out which ad produces the higher CTR and converts better into goal completion. This process never ends; as soon as one ad has been beaten (and becomes the new A), you put up a new B ad to compete against it. You will need at least one different A/B split ad group for each of your main product or service campaigns. So if you have 20 products, that's at least 40 different ads. Each of these ad groups may be associated with hundreds of keywords. It's a lot of work, but worth it.

Visit the "campaign summary" category of the "campaign management" tab and click on your first ad group. Select the "ad variations" tab on the far right and add one B ad to make up your first A/B pair. You will remember that we earlier selected "show ads evenly over time" and "display better-performing ads more often." This was designed to cater for these split tests, which Google will now essentially automate for you.

5.3 Landing page optimization

Now we turn to the most important area of your paid campaign: your quality score (QS for short). I use the quality triangle to explain the concept, consisting of three points:

✧ <u>Phrase match text</u> – the main phrase category you have chosen for each ad group, for example "mutual fund."

✧ <u>Ad text copy</u> – the repetition of the main phrase category (or shorter variants of it) in your ad headline, description, and target URL.

✧ <u>Landing page copy</u> – repetition of the main phrase category in the landing page title, description, heading tags, and other on-page elements.

The Google Adwords team incorporates quality assessment of landing pages into the process of calculating advertisers' minimum bids. The help file tells you:

> We believe high quality ads attract more clicks, encourage user trust and result in better long term performance. To encourage relevant and successful ads within AdWords, our system defines a Quality Score to set your keyword status, minimum CPC bid and ad rank for the ad auction.

So what does all this mean? Really it's very simple. If your ads simply point to your homepage, and that page looks very different from your ad, then it will cost you more to serve each and every ad. Yes, that's right – the auction is rigged and others can rank better than you while paying less per click.

Of course, you suffer in other ways. If a user clicks on a very specific ad like "Quality Mutual Fund" then simply gets taken to the homepage of a big financial services company, from which they have to navigate four more clicks to find the product, the chances are they just give up, meaning that you have paid for the click but get very poor conversion.

To counter this double whammy of poor quality and poor conversion combined with high CPC, do the following:

✧ Use the phrase you are matching against in the ad headline.

✧ Repeat the phrase (or a subset of it) in the ad description.

✧ Use the phrase in the target URL of the landing page.

✧ Use the phrase in the title of the landing page.

✧ Use an <h1> tag at the top of the page that repeats the ad headline exactly.

✧ Use an <h2> tag immediately below, which repeats the ad description.

✧ Follow both with well-written copy that repeats the phrase and related terms.

✧ Funnel the user quickly from there to a money page in your site.

✧ Reference all landing pages from the HTML and XML sitemaps of the site.

As an example, let's walk through the mutual fund example step by step:

1 User types the search query "mutual fund."

2 User sees an ad in the following format:

> High Quality Mutual Fund
> Top performing fund in last 5 years
> Rewards those saving for retirement
> *http://www.yourdomain.com*

3 User clicks on the ad and is taken to the following (target) URL:
http://www.yourdomain.com/mutual-funds/retirement.html

4 The title and description of the page she sees are as follows:

> Title: High Quality Mutual Fund from ABC Company Inc.
> Description: Find out how this top performing mutual fund can help you save for retirement.

5 The page copy she sees is a slightly longer version of this:

> <h1> tag: High Quality Mutual Fund
> <h2> tag: Top performing fund in last 5 years
> Body text: The Grow Better Fund from ABC Co Inc. has

topped the five-year Mutual Fund performance chart within the high income category of the Morningstar tables for 2006 and 2007. $1,000 invested on 1 December 2005 was worth $1,456 on 1 December 2007.

<h2> tag: Rewards those saving for retirement
Body text: The Grow Better Mutual Fund is perfect for those nearing retirement who are seeking high income at moderate financial risk. You could join thousands of savers who are already benefiting from the work of our top performing investment team.

<h2> tag: Download a Prospectus Now
Body Text: To find out more, visit our <u>Grow Better Profile Page</u> and download a prospectus.

6 She is impressed: the landing page delivers on the promise made in the ad. She visits the money page and downloads the prospectus.

So can you find out what your quality score for any given keyword is? The answer, you will be relieved to hear, is yes. However, Google doesn't make it that easy for you to find. Go to your ad group and click on the "customize columns" links. Select "show quality score" from the drop-down. You will see one of three ratings, which mean the following:

✧ <u>Great</u>. Your keyword is very relevant and your QS needs no further improvement. This is what you are aiming for on every line.
✧ <u>OK</u>. Your keyword is relevant, but you could still benefit from a higher QS and further quality triangle refinements.
✧ <u>Poor</u>. This keyword is not very relevant to users and Google suggests that you replace it with a more specific keyword. If, alternatively, you wish to continue using this keyword, you should further optimize either your ad copy, your landing page content, or both.

To get every single keyword up to a "great" score, you may find that you need to create a separate landing page for each and every ad group. I would certainly recommend this, as your conversions will also improve if you take the time.

This may all sound rather exhausting, and indeed it can be. However, once you've got this stuff right you will benefit from it long into the future, in terms of lower costs per click, increased conversion rates, and return on investment.

5.4 Campaign management

Campaign management is all about tweaking and continually improving your budget, day parting, bids, and ad variations to maximize the cost and return on investment of your campaigns. There's more to it than you might think!

Choosing the best position for your ad

If you cast your mind back to the SERPs and snippets section (page 118), you will remember that Google serves up to three ads at the top of the SERPs, then a further eight down the righthand side. You will perhaps also remember the F-shaped heat map of where users' eyes go as they peruse the page. Many advertisers only want to be in one place: number one. However, that costs: The bid curve for any keyphrase (and particularly popular ones) climbs inexorably as you near position one.

If your budget is more modest, why not look at the oft-overlooked position 4? Or the much-maligned position 8? Position 4 is where the user's eyes rest when they finish scanning the first line. Position 8 is where their eyes linger when they move their mouse to the scrollbar (i.e., to scroll down through the results). You can in fact ask for a particular position and, although Google may not always honor your request, this can be a very effective way of keeping down your costs.

Setting your maximum bid level

Many unsophisticated Adwords users set a default bid cost and leave that to apply to all their ads. Google will, of course, charge you less than this if your bid is winning the auction. However, you do not play in isolation. I have seen many customers enter a bidding war with their competitors, driving CPC ever higher and sharing the pain through their maximum bids.

I always recommend that clients set their bids individually for each keyphrase and continually compare this to their average CPC, average position, and number of ads served. Keep ticking the bid up in small increments until you are happy with where you are. Drop the bid occasionally to see what happens.

Bear in mind that many advertisers set daily budget limits that they exhaust every day. However, many shoppers only get online quite late in the evening, after they have put the kids to bed or cleared their chores for the day. Why not set a day parting on your more competitive terms for the hours of 10 p.m. onward? You may find that you have less competition at this time, due to other advertisers dropping out of the race.

In the CPC and keyword dialogue in Adwords, you can enter a number of bid-control parameters all at once:

> "luxury business cards" ** 0.04 **
> http://www.chambersprint.com/ business-printing/business-
> cards/luxury-business-cards.html ** #6-8

The above syntax will, all in one go:

- ✧ Set the maximum bid for the phrase match "luxury business cards" at $0.04.
- ✧ Set the landing URL for that keyphrase.
- ✧ Request position 6–8 for the ad in the SERPs.

Monitoring your click-through rate

While there is no hard-and-fast rule, a click-through rate (CTR) of
1.8–3.5% is in an acceptable range (and anything over that represents a
very good performance). If your ad achieves less than 0.5% CTR,
Google may well delist it. The lower your CTR%, the more you will have
to pay in cost per click (CPC) to get into the top three or four results for
your chosen keywords (vital if you want to appear on partner sites like
AOL). Keep an eye on these numbers and rotate your A/B pairs
ruthlessly.

Working the long tail

Remember Sam Larder from our earlier section (page 37), with the ski-
in–ski-out chalet in Verbier? He used to target "ski chalet" and "chalet
verbier," but now focuses on "ski chalet crèche" and "ski chalet child
care," as they cost him less and convert better, given his proximity to the
local crèche. Don't forget this lesson in your own paid campaigns.
Perhaps it isn't really necessary, after all, to take on the big boys for the
top spot on major keywords.

Avoiding click fraud

Click fraud is a huge issue in the world of pay-per-click advertising. It
occurs when advertisers seek to exhaust the budgets of their competitors
through repeatedly clicking their ads (or paying cheap labor in China or
India to do so). This can involve huge sums. In 2006, for example,
Google agreed a $90 million settlement on a click-fraud suit filed by
Lane's Gifts and Collectibles.

   If you are planning to spend large sums on PPC advertising, it
would be unwise to do so without some suitable click-fraud monitoring
software. There are different types of tools commercially available.
Some work by blocking repeated clicks from the same IP address, with

a warning screen displayed instead warning the offender that their activity will be reported. Others simply track and audit the behavior in the back end, to support a claim back to Google.

I do not recommend any particular tool, but you are welcome to discuss the issue with fellow webmasters on the forum (www.seo-expert-services.co.uk) and learn from them how best to combat it.

Step 6: Making the Map

This chapter is all about local search optimization. Over the last few years, all the major search engines have invested in both regional and local search and mapping capabilities. The challenges include ranking well in regional language pages (e.g., pages in Spanish), ranking well in regional search instances (e.g., pages from Mexico), showing up on Google Earth and Google Map services, and scoring well on regular searches that have locally qualified search terms.

6.1 Language optimization

At time of writing, Google supports more than 104 languages or dialects. In China alone, it is available in simple Chinese, traditional Chinese, Mongolian, and Uighur. In India, Google is available in Hindi, Bengali, Telugu, Marathi, and Tamil. There are even Google language instances for Esperanto, Elmer Fudd, and Klingon. Someone has far too much time on their hands!

As SEO remains a relatively immature profession, the presence of truly global SEO firms with multilanguage capability is still relatively rare. In my own business I partner with leading SEO experts in countries around the world and use their services, as associates, for international campaigns. I have, for example, undertaken SEO campaigns in China and India.

Many Google search instances have a radio button that users can select to obtain only results in a certain language. For example, on Google France (google.fr) you can select "Pages Francophones" to narrow down results to pages in French.

You can use metadata to specify the natural language (or languages) of your website. You can only have one language for a user agent (e.g., a web browser) but multiple languages on one page for the human visitor.

For example, you might have a Canadian homepage that declares English to the browser but has both English and French text on the actual page.

The languages are specified through a two-letter code, such as "en" for English and "es" for Spanish. One or more hyphenated values can be tacked on to the initial two-letter code to specify regional or ethnic variations, such as "en-us" for US English and "zh-cmn" for Mandarin Chinese. To find the appropriate code for your language, type ISO639 into Google and check out the results. To find the right hyphenated sub-tag, search on the IANA registry and RFC 4646.

To be absolutely sure that Google interprets the language of your pages correctly, you need to ensure that you:

✧ Reference language in your <HTML> tag.
✧ Reference language in your meta tags.
✧ If you need to use other languages on your page, first preface them with their own language tags.

So if for example your Canadian webpage is primarily in English and you wish it to be recognized as such, but you have a short welcome phrase in French halfway down the page, you might use the following:

Before the <head> tag:
<HTML lang="en-US">

Between the <head> tags:
<META http-equiv="Content-Language" content="en-US">

Between the <body> Tags, where the welcome text is to be:
<p lang="en-US">Welcome</p>
<p lang="fr-CA">Bienvenue</p>

Note that your <HTML> tag may contain a lot more information, but as long as the lang declaration appears somewhere in there, you will be fine.

In the above example, the <HTML> tag tells Google that the page (from a human user perspective) will be mainly in the US dialect of English. The <meta> tag tells any browser to display the page in US English. The lang="fr-CA" attribute in the <p> tag tells Google that the text in that tag is in Canadian French.

Once your page has been correctly recognized by Google as being in the right language, the rest of your SEO battle is all about how well optimized you are for importance, relevance, and text matching to the search query. It is not possible for one page in French to be more French than another!

6.2 Geographical optimization

You will note that Google.de has both "Seiten auf Deutsch" (pages in German) and "Seiten aus Deutschland" (pages from Germany). There is a reason for this difference. Any multinational company is likely to have a site that is based in one country but contains pages in many different languages.

A country code top-level domain (ccTLD) is used and reserved for a country or dependent territory, as distinct from a generic top-level domain (gTLD) such as .com, .net, or .org. At time of writing Google has 113 ccTLDs, including Google.co.uk (UK), Google.de (Germany), and Google.fr (France). It has encouraged the uptake of local instances through wide distribution of the Google Toolbar (which encourages users to set their local instance of Google as the search index used by the Toolbar).

Some local search instances are less well developed, particularly in smaller or developing countries. For example, Google.com.jm (Jamaica) only has 119,000 pages indexed with a .com.jm ccTLD and local searchers have yet to develop a strong culture of using their home search instance. There is no "pages from Jamaica" option.

Similarly, the .us ccTLD has been available for registration since 1985 to US citizens, residents, or organizations, or a foreign entity with a presence in the US. However, most US webmasters use the .com gTLD and the Google.com interface has no "pages from the US" option.

Elsewhere in the world, ranking well on a local instance is of great importance to webmasters. For example, research has shown that 3.5 times as many searchers in the UK use Google.co.uk as do Google.com and of these, 35–45% regularly check the "pages from the UK" radio button to narrow down their search. Ranking near the top of these narrowed local results is thus a pretty important mission for an online business.

However, site owners in some countries (particularly the UK and Canada) have found getting the correct local instance presence somewhat challenging. I will use Google.co.uk as an example in this section and walk you through some of key steps required to rank well in the "pages from the UK" option.

Use or switch to a ccTLD domain name

This may seem a little obvious. However, many webmasters are attracted to the international connotations that go along with yourdomain.com. The problem is that Google struggles to identify the country of origin of a .com TLD correctly. So moving to .co.uk, .org.uk, .ltd.uk, or even the obscure .me.uk might be of long-term benefit for those with a solely UK audience or customer base.

While all of the other steps below should help (particularly the next one), there is simply no guarantee that the homepage of a .com domain will ever rank well on Google.co.uk as things currently stand. Starting without a .co.uk domain is like starting a chess game without your queen!

Put your site on a locally hosted server

If you do insist on using a .com domain name, it is particularly important that your site is hosted in the UK. This is the only factor that I have empirically proven Google to use in classifying the country of your site correctly.

Hosting in the UK may not be as simple as you assume. As I noted on page 69, 1and1.co.uk, one of the biggest UK hosting providers, actually has its data center located in Germany. If you have an existing site, you can find out its IP address and hosting location from Netcraft using the following URL syntax:

http://toolbar.netcraft.com/site_report?url=http://www.yourdomain.com

Without a UK-based IP address, your .com site will certainly not be indexed in the "pages from the UK" section of Google. For example, were you hosted with 1and1, your site would actually appear in the "Seiten aus Deutschland" section of Google.de.

Obtain links from predominantly local sites

There is much reliable evidence that having a more than proportionate number of inbound links from other UK-based sites will help improve Google.co.uk rankings. To obtain such inbound links, you can use a mixture of link-exchange, directory-submission, and link-baiting techniques (covered in further depth in the off-page optimization section, page 132, and the Web 2.0 section, page 166).

Free, paid, and reciprocal directory submissions form by far the most reliable technique. An example of a UK-based directory is the PR5-ranked Abrexa, which offers a paid listing for £9.95 (covering both Abrexa and its sister site, Limey Search).

FORUM TOOLS The UK is relatively underserved by directories when compared to the US and paid listings are on the expensive side. However, you should not let this put you off. On the forum (www.seo-expert-services.co.uk) I maintain a master list of over 100 UK-based directories that offer either free, reciprocal, or paid links. By building up these links, you should ensure that your site performs bet-

ter on Google.co.uk. The ten top directories below should get you
started.

Directory name	Directory URL	PR
Applegate	www.applegate.co.uk	6 (B2B sites only)
FreeIndex	www.freeindex.co.uk	6
Lifestyle UK	www.lifestyle.co.uk	6
Ozami	www.ozami.co.uk	6
Splut	www.splut.co.uk	6
B2B Index	www.b2index.co.uk	5
Top Local Listings	www.toplocallistings.co.uk	5
UK Business Directory	www.business-directory-uk.co.uk	5
HaaBaa	www.haabaa.co.uk	4
The Big Web Directory	www.bigwebdirectory.com	4

Other, more traditional directories are also worth a look, such as
yell.com, Thomson Local, TheBestOf, and TouchLocal.

Sign up for Google Maps

I cover this in greater depth in the next section (page 213). While there
is no evidence, at the time of writing, that a Google Maps listing has any
bearing on the main index rankings, it seems logical that it may do in
the future. For this reason, I recommend that all my clients obtain an
address-verified entry in Google Maps.

Use localized metadata on your pages

To reinforce your other activity (and to help with other search engines
such as MSN and Yahoo!), I recommend including various key local
meta tags between the <head> tags of your homepage. I suggest using:

```
<meta name="country" content="United Kingdom">
<meta name="geo.country" content="GB" />
```

And either of the following:

```
<meta name="geo.position" content="51.4998;-0.1246" />
<meta name="ICBM" content="51.4998;-0.1246" />
```

The 51.5012;-0.1258 (latitude;longitude) example references (for the geo.position and ICBM tags) are for the Houses of Parliament in Central London. To get your own coordinates, I suggest putting your business postcode into Multimap, getting up the results page, and reading off the longitude and latitude coordinates from the Map Information section below the map. To test it out for our example, the postcode for the Houses of Parliament is SW1A 0AA, so try using the URL:

http://www.multimap.com/map/browse.cgi?pc=SW1A0AA

Each country has its own geo-positioning solution. In the US, the best service to use to do the same job is http://geocoder.us/ (so the ICBM tag for 1600 Pennsylvania Ave, Washington DC would be 38.898748, -77.037684). Incidentally, the acronym ICBM stands for inter-continental ballistic missile and is a bit of a throwback to the days of the Cold War. It's a good job that these days the Russians are more likely to use ICBM coordinates to locate the White House in Google Earth than to drop a bomb on it!

As with Google Maps, while there is no great evidence that any of these locational meta tags makes a big difference today to your local instance ranking, there is a chance that search engines may make greater use of them in the future. For this reason, I always recommend them to any clients with local optimization needs.

Use HTML address tags on your page

Not many webmasters are either aware of or use the address tag. Unlike the meta tags above, the content in the address tag will actually render on your page (and should thus be included within the <body> section, most likely near the bottom of your homepage).

Anything placed within the address tags will usually render in your browser in italics, with a line break before and after the address text. If you want line breaks within the address, you need to enter these yourself. So as an example (with a line break after "Square"):

<ADDRESS>Parliamentary Bookshop, 12 Bridge Street, Parliament Square.
London SW1A 2JX, United Kingdom.</ADDRESS>

would render in your browser roughly like this:

Parliamentary Bookshop, 12 Bridge Street, Parliament Square.
London SW1A 2JX, United Kingdom.

Again, there is no conclusive evidence that use of address tags alone make much of a difference to local instance rankings, although several webmasters have reported good results from use of these tags in conjunction with other measures.

All of this takes time to work through. Correcting the position of your site in local instance rankings may take up to six months, particularly if you have a new site that has only recently been registered as a domain. Patience is a real virtue here! Sometimes people make changes only to reverse them in frustration before they take effect. Another problem is when good things happen but webmasters have no idea which of their actions caused the benign effect. Trust me, have patience, and in time you will see the rewards.

The growth of the internet in China and Russia

Russia is one of the world's fastest-growing economies and is the most heavily populated country in Europe. Internet penetration currently stands at just 19.5% (compared to 69.9% in the US). In China, penetration is just 10.9%, although given that its population is more than four times that of the US the absolute numbers are still large. The penetration levels in western Europe and North America appear to have stabilized and look unlikely to grow significantly in the future, so the majority of new world-wide internet users will come from fast-developing areas such as India and China, while the bulk of new European users are likely to hail from Russia. Within 18 months, China will overtake the US as the biggest internet community online.

In China Google enjoys only a 27% market share, very much second fiddle to Baidu with 55%. Similarly, in Russia Google is in third place, with Yandex the clear leader. How do you get listed in these two important and growing challengers to Google's dominance?

Getting listed on Baidu

Unlike Google, Baidu (www.baidu.com) merges its organic results with results from its paid listings service. As such, the quickest way to achieve a top ranking on Baidu is to participate in its paid service. As there is not (yet) an English-language Baidu ads interface, it is best to use an agent.

To rank well organically, you must first realize that the Chinese search audience is very sino-centric. Your target landing page must be fully in Chinese and presented in the Chinese style. This, inevitably, means using the services of a Chinese translator (and quite possibly a web designer too). Note that Simplified Chinese will be sufficient to serve all markets. The entire web page should be encoded using a Simplified Chinese language declaration in the metadata of the page:

Between the <head> tags:
<META http-equiv="Content-Language" content="zh-CN">

When ready, you can submit your site to Baidu from the following page:

http://www.baidu.com/search/url_submit.html

Once listed on Baidu, you can improve your position by sourcing high-quality inbound links from Chinese directories. Many of the best directories to target are those based in Taiwan and Hong Kong, where internet penetration has been higher for longer. To get started, try the following three:

Directory name	Directory URL	Costs	PageRank
Cooperative Directory	www.webdirectory.com.tw	Free	4
Taiwan Directory	www.taiwandirectory.com/tw	Free	4
Web Guide Hong Kong	www.index.webstudio.com.hk	Free	3

There is further help available from my forum, should you need it.

Getting listed on Yandex

Yandex (www.yandex.com) does not accept site submissions from sites hosted outside Russia. This does not mean, however, that domain names have to end in .ru (Russia) or .ua (Ukraine). In fact, any site with an IP address in a Russian-speaking country or with pages in Russian will eventually be indexed by the search engine. Try comparing a search on Yandex for "Intel" with a search for "Amazon." You will note that Intel, which has a part of its site in Russian, fares better in the results than Amazon.

So the first rule to learn for Yandex is to have some text in Russian. Generally, it will be best to enclose any Russian-language text with the correct W3C markup. For example, the following Russian phrase (roughly equivalent to "the early bird catches the worm") would be coded as follows:

<span lang="RU">ранняя пташка червяка ловит</span>

The second rule is that your page will be indexed by Yandex more quickly if it is linked to by sites that are hosted in Russia. Personally, I recommend that clients seek listings on five or six quality Russia-based bilingual directories. The following three sites will get you started:

Directory name	Directory URL	Costs	PageRank
Russia on the Net	www.ru/eng	Free	6
Tickets of Russia	www.ticketsofrussia.ru/russia	Free	4
Rusmarket	www.rusmarket.com	$99 p.a.	5

Again, there is further help available from my forum, should you need it.

6.3 Google Maps and Google Earth

Before we turn to the most popular of Google's geographical information services (GIS), Google Maps and Google Earth, it is worth mentioning that there may be more Google products in this space than you are aware of. For example:

✧ Google Ride Finder plots the location of participating taxi and limousine services in major US cities, including San Francisco and Chicago.

✧ Google Transit is a web application through which users can plan their trip across the public transport network of certain US cities, including Seattle, Tampa, and Pittsburgh. The service calculates route, transit time, and cost, and can compare the trip to the automobile equivalent.

✧ Google Street View provides 360-degree panoramic, street-level views of New York, Miami, Denver, and more. There are even maps of other planets at Google Moon and Google Mars!

At the moment this might all seem a little gimmicky. However, this commitment to GIS shows that Google means business in this area. As the web increasingly goes mobile, served through high-powered handheld smartphones and PDAs, local information, routing, and mapping services are likely to become the killer search apps of the future.

Optimizing for Google Maps

Google Maps is located at www.maps.google.com. The service is multilayered and what you can do with the maps varies by location:

✧ Partial mapping service only, which does not include detail down to a street level. For example in China at the time of writing, Google Maps only provides highway and passenger rail coverage. In India, there is street coverage for most major cities but only highway coverage elsewhere.

✧ Mapping service only, countries that have maps that are detailed down to street level but currently enjoy no further services (e.g., Belgium, New Zealand, and Thailand).

✧ Advanced mapping services, countries that have maps to street level and where users can undertake more advanced functions. For example, business owners can add their listings to the service, users can search at street level, and driving directions can be obtained. Example countries include the UK, the US, France, and Germany.

In this section I am going to focus on the business listings service, as this is the most important aspect of Google Maps from an optimization perspective.

You may have noticed that Google sometimes gives you a map at the top of the regular SERPs, with three results alongside it. This happens when the searcher has included in their search query both a recognized place name and a recognized local search service or service category. These results are drawn from the Google Maps database.

To see how this works, try typing "restaurant Little Rock" into the main Google search box. A map appears top left under the title "Local results for **restaurant** near **Little Rock**, AR, USA." There are three results alongside and Google places three markers on the map at the exact location of the restaurants.

Now try opening another browser window or tab and performing a search on "Little Rock." Open the resulting map in the Google Maps service and zoom in. You will note that the center of Little Rock (as far as Google is concerned) is the corner of Broadway and West Markham Street. Now click on the "Find businesses" tab and enter "restaurant" in the search box on the left. The same three restaurants you saw before will get added to the map, along with a further seven. By now, you should have spotted the key factor used to generate the rankings: the top three results are the restaurant businesses closest to what Google sees as the center of Little Rock.

You may well ask where all these listings come from. The answer is more complex then you might suppose, as it involves a merging of base data from business directory companies and address-verified listings submitted by business owners.

In the US, Google Maps draws its base data from a variety of Yellow Pages sources, although it does not reveal which. Based on my research, much of the address data is sourced from Acxiom (whose data set can be best observed at www.allpages.com) and other data, including reviews, comes from insiderpages.com, 10best.com, wcities.com, citysearch.com, judysbook.com, and Yahoo! travel. In the UK, Google has used, at different times, both Yell.com and Thomson Local. Other data comes from a number of sources including, for restaurants, Restaurant-guide.com, Toptable.co.uk, and TimeOut.com.

Whatever the origins of your base data, you will be relieved to find that you can take over your business listing, if it's there already, or create it from scratch if it does not yet exist. The easiest way to start is to create a totally new entry, which you can later request to be merged with your existing entry if appropriate.

First, if you do not already have a Google account, sign up for one at https://www.google.com/accounts/NewAccount. Then sign in to Google Maps (at www.maps.google.com) with your new log-in details. Finally, access the local business center from the "Add or edit your business" link, click on the "Add New Listing" link, and enter your details.

Once you have completed your entry, Google will send you a pincode by regular surface mail to the recorded address associated with the site submitted. Once you have revisited the Google Maps listing for your site and added the pincode, your address is verified and the site added to Google Maps.

As a footnote, if you wish to remove an old, out-of-date business address where you can no longer receive mail, you will find this very difficult to do. The best way to tackle this is to ensure that all the phone books and Yellow Pages directories that used to list your old address have removed this out-of-date information from their database. Eventually, your old data will drop out of Google's results during a data upload.

To return to Little Rock for a moment, the way in which Google Maps works has interesting implications for the future of search. For locally qualified search queries, the best way to be found in future may well be to have a properly classified business location very close to the center of the nearest major town or city. Note that any business can validly have more than one branch listed in the database. It will be interesting to see how many businesses acquire, for example, a tiny garage or lock-up, just to have a valid address in the center of town. Will virtual office providers find a new revenue stream from businesses listing a branch in their city-center office blocks?

So, what do I suggest from an SEO perspective? First, you need to ensure that you have correctly classified your business in the Google Maps database. By correctly classified, I mean that you have selected the single category that best describes your main service and is searched on most often by users. Secondly, you should use a branch address close to the center of the nearest local center of population or county/region (even if this means acquiring a virtual office address). Thirdly, you should consider acquiring multiple branch addresses and listing these under different categories, particularly if your business offers multiple products and services and/or serves multiple local markets.

Can I emphasize the ethics of this? You should never do anything in search, as I have said before, that is designed to mislead the user or misrepresent your business. If you do, your competitors will be the first to write to Google about it and you will get what you deserve if Google decides to penalize your site. However, you should not confuse ethics with fair competition. If you genuinely serve multiple locations with multiple products and are prepared to pay for a local business presence, then get stuck in!

Optimizing for Google Earth

Google Earth is a virtual globe program that superimposes images obtained from satellite imagery, aerial photography, and geographical information systems (GIS) onto a 3D globe. The application has become very popular with web users worldwide, keen to see what their house looks like from space.

You might be wondering what on (Google) earth I am on about when I suggest that you should consider carefully the potential optimization opportunities here. However, it seems inevitable to me that Google Earth will be available in future not as a standalone application but as a web-based interface. After all, this is already possible at www.flashearth.com (an unofficial and experimental service that uses data from Google and others without permission) and Wikimapia (www.wikimapia.org). As bandwidth continues to improve, Google Earth will inevitably one day become the top-level interface for the Google Maps service.

To futureproof yourself, I recommend the creation of individual Keyhole Markup Language (KML) files for all your business addresses. KML supports the display of three-dimensional geospatial data in Google Earth, Google Maps, and other similar programs. A simple KML file for the Statue of Liberty in New York might look something like this:

```
<?xml version="1.0" encoding="UTF-8"?>
<kml xmlns="http://earth.google.com/kml/2.0">
<Placemark>
  <description>Statue of Liberty</description>
  <name> Statue of Liberty</name>
  <Point>
    <coordinates>-74.044700, 40.689400</coordinates>
  </Point>
</Placemark>
</kml>
```

Each <Placemark> tag defines a location and the precise coordinates are included within the <Point> tags. Note that unlike meta tags where latitude comes first, followed by longitude, KML tags define longitude first, then latitude. Get them the wrong way around and your place-holder is likely to end up in the middle of an ocean somewhere!

To test your Statue of Liberty KML file, download the Google Earth application, save the KML file to your desktop, then double-click on the KML file to launch Google Earth and take you to a PlaceMark for the famous New York landmark. The Statue of Liberty is one of the locations in Google Earth that is represented in 3D, so is quite a good demonstration of the power of the software.

What you should do is create a keyword-rich description of your business locations, then build a KML file for each in turn. Save the KML files to the root directory of your website (i.e., http://www.yourdomain.com/ location-1.kml). Finally, add a line of code for each location to your sitemap file, so that Google will index your location data when next it crawls your sitemap:

```
<url>
  <loc>http://www.yourdomain.com/location-1.kml</loc>
</url>
<url>
  <loc>http://www.yourdomain.com/location-2.kml</loc>
</url>
```

After a few days, you will find that when you visit Google Earth and zoom in on the location where your branch is, a placeholder appears for your business on the map. This data will also be accessible through the "user created content" subset of Google Maps.

The KML schema actually supports quite a wide range of customization, which you can use to enhance the appearance of the description box in both Google Maps and Google Earth. The example overleaf for my own business places in the location entry a small picture of the building, a link to the business website, the business address, links to a contact form, and links to other branches and their maps.

The final step is to add a link to Google Maps from the locations, branch finder, or contact us page of your website, which follows a particular dynamic URL syntax. For example, to code the link to the KML file opposite, you would use:

```
<a href="http://maps.google.com/maps?f=q&hl=en&q=http://
www.seo-expert-services.co.uk/seo-expert-services-
london.kml">SEO Expert Services – London Branch Map</a>
```

```xml
<?xml version="1.0" encoding="UTF-8"?>
<kml xmlns="http://earth.google.com/kml/2.1">
  <Document>
    <Placemark>
      <name>SEO Expert Services - London</name>
      <description>
       <![CDATA[
        <DIV>
            <img src="http://www.seo-expert-
services.co.uk/images/stories/london-office.jpg" alt="SEO
Expert Services - London Office" width="160"
height="116" /><br>
            <h3>Expert Search Engine Optimization
Worldwide</h3>
            <A href="http://www.seo-expert-
services.co.uk/about-us/seo-consulting-division.html">SEO
Expert Services - London</A>
            </DIV>
            <DIV>
            Portland House <BR>Stag Place<br>
            London SW1E 5RS<br>United
Kingdom<br> <br>
            <A href="http://www.seo-expert-services.co.uk/
contact.html">Contact Us</A><br><br>
            <h3>Other Branches:</h3>
            <A href="http://www.seo-expert-
services.co.uk/about-us/seo-delivery-division.html">SEO
Expert Services - India</A>   [<A
href="http://www.seo-expert-services.co.uk/seo-expert-
services-india.kml">map</a>]<br>
            <A href="http://www.seo-expert-
services.co.uk/about-us/ses-china-seo.html">SEO Expert
Services - China</A>   [<A
href="http://www.seo-expert-services.co.uk/seo-expert-
services-china.kml">map</a>]
        </DIV>
       ]]>
      </description>
      <Point>
       <coordinates>-0.141584,51.497369</coordinates>
      </Point>
    </Placemark>
  </Document>
</kml>
```

Now both Google and website users will be able to use your KML data to find your business locations. In the future, as Google Earth and Google Maps come closer together, so your optimization of your local presence information will improve.

There are three other ways to put your business on the map using the geographic web. Launch Google Earth and open the Layers > Geographic Web section. You should see tick boxes for Best of Google Earth Community, Panoramio, and Wikipedia. New Google Earth downloads set Panoramio and Wikipedia as default layers.

The function of <u>Panoramio</u> (now part of Google) is for users to upload their photographs, together with the coordinates at which they took them. The Google Panoramio layer overlays small thumbnails of the photographs onto Google Earth. You could, should you choose, sign up for Panoramio and upload a photograph of your premises or a picture of your products. Add the correct coordinates and your picture will appear as an overlay on the Google Earth view of your location.

If your business is of sufficient size and notability to have its own <u>Wikipedia</u> entry, you could geotag the Wikipedia article so that it shows up in Google Earth. The easiest way to do this is by using one of the "[[coor title d[ms]]]" or "[[coor at d[ms]]]" templates on Wikipedia, anywhere within the article text.

For example, if you search for La Tzoumaz (a beautiful Swiss ski resort) on Wikipedia, you will (at the moment at least) find the following text in the center of the article:

Coordinates: 46.14469669243357° N 7.23305940628051 8° E

The wiki markup that achieves this is:

Coordinates: {{coor at d|46.14469669243357|N|
7.23305940628051 8|E|region:CH-VS_type:city}}

So much of good SEO is getting ahead of the game. As new developments appear you should always get your entry in early before the rest of the crowd descend en masse. While Google Earth is currently fairly nascent technology, its place in the future of search (particularly as the web goes mobile) is likely to be significant.

6.4 Priming for local search

It is important not to neglect good, old-fashioned, locally qualified search optimization. In simple terms, a search on Google for "indian restaurant little rock" will still serve (underneath the one-box extract from Google Maps) the best-placed organic results for that search from the main Google index. In your SEO activities you should still ensure that your homepage and at least one landing page on your site are well optimized for relevant search queries. This means having your place name prominent in heading tags and other on-page text blocks and having anchor-rich inbound links from other sites that include the place name.

You don't need to go overboard on this. Just a few inbound deep links to your landing page and one or two to your homepage should be enough to ensure decent rankings for most queries.

One really great example of local search priming is wedding photographers. In my professional experience I have encountered a number of photographers who could make a very good second income as SEO experts. They have cornered the search market for "wedding photographer Toronto" or "wedding photographer Seattle."

Typically, their sites include lots of pictures of local landmarks or wedding venues (so lots of relevant text matches) and they have obtained multiple keyword-rich inbound links including the area they serve.

These guys (and girls) know what they are doing! They only want to work locally and they are always busy as a result of their SEO endeavors. If you have a very locally oriented, typically service-based business, why not copy their example?

Phase 3

Ongoing maintenance

Step 7: Tracking and tuning

A search engine optimization and promotion strategy is not a one-off task but an ongoing and iterative process, where you tweak and refine toward ever better rankings. In doing so it is vital that you objectively monitor your performance, using measurable indicators and statistics.

In a way, the data you can obtain from Google Analytics can be seen as similar to your profit and loss account, and the information gleaned from other tools is more like your marketing plan. While performance assessment is useful, however, it is best not to become too obsessed with it or to get carried away with analysis – the time is better spent actually running your business.

7.1 Google Analytics

Google Analytics is a superb toolset and is simply a must-have for any webmaster. Its functionality includes visitor tracking (new and repeat), traffic sources (search engine and website referrer), visitor location, visitor behavior, visitor trends, and much, much more. The information is gathered from a simple piece of Javascript placed near the footer in the HTML of each of your pages. I will discuss its most relevant functions here, but there is plenty more for you to explore.

Installing Google Analytics

Installing Google Analytics is very straightforward. First, visit www.google.com/analytics and register using your Google account (if you don't yet have a Google account, see page 187). Next, enter the URL of the first site you would like to track. Google provides you with a unique Javascript code snippet, which you need to place in the template file of your website software or manually add to each page.

As soon as the Javascript is in place tracking begins, and the sheer depth of information it provides leaves little to be desired. Unlike other free visitor trackers, which often force the use of annoying and amateurish badges or buttons, Google Analytics simply runs quietly in the background, gathering the necessary information without any visible signs of its presence.

Basic keyword reporting

Google Analytics does a very good job of recording the keyphrases used in each and every search referral to your site. By drilling down through the results, it is possible to identify terms that might warrant further optimization. Sometimes you may be surprised by how people find your site. Access this function from the Traffic sources > Keywords menu function.

While the basic elements of Google Analytics are pretty impressive, the higher functions of the service are where it really comes into its own.

Customer journey tracking

Each customer journey through your site can be broken down into the following four stages, each of which can be tracked using Google Analytics:

- ✧ Landing page. While some of your return visitors will enter your site by typing the site address directly into their browser, all your new visitors will find you through either a search engine, a PPC advert, or an inbound link from another site. They begin their journey on a landing page.
- ✧ Funnel path. Funnels define the specific path you expect a visitor to take through your site to achieve each of your goals. Funnelling is the process of moving your user from landing page to information gathering to money page, building commitment

through the process. Each goal has its own funnel and each can be tracked separately in Google Analytics.

✧ Money page. The money page is where the user has the opportunity to complete one of your goals, be it to download a brochure or purchase a product.

✧ Goal completion. Once the user has completed a goal, it is best practice to send them to a confirmation or thank-you page, where there are details, for example, of how long they can expect to wait for product delivery. With Google Analytics, this page can be associated with the end of the funnel and a monetary value for return-on-investment (ROI) analysis.

You can set up to four goals per site by selecting "Analytics settings" from the top left of the Google Analytics interface, then clicking on the "Edit" link to the right of the URL of your tracked site. This accesses the profile setting for that URL from where both goals and funnels can be defined, including a monetary value for each goal completed.

Let's use Brad's business as an illustration of what can be achieved. We'll assume that he has paid for links on two well-trafficked ezines for small business owners. He has paid a total of $500 for the links and wants to track the performance and ROI of these, both in total and by individual ezine. The paid links point to a specific landing page on his site that he has set up solely for the purpose of this campaign. On the page, he provides a coupon code offering 50% off business cards for readers of the ezines.

Brad's first step is to have the ezine webmasters include a campaign tracking parameter (of "ezines") in the link HTML, as follows:

```
<a href="http://www.chambersprint.com/business-cards-half-price-
offer.html?utm_medium=paidlinks&utm_campaign=ezines"
rel="nofollow">50% off Business Cards</a>
```

Note that Brad has asked each webmaster to include a "nofollow" parameter in the link. This means that Google will not follow the link to that page or include the link when calculating PageRank. He has done this for two reasons. First, he does not want to risk a penalty from Google for buying links. Secondly, he does not want search engines to index the page; this is an offer code he wants only readers of the ezine to find. He reinforces this by instructing crawlers not to index this page (using disallow in his robots.txt file).

The next step is for Brad to set up the campaign in Google Analytics and define the funnel to goal completion that he expects ezine readers to follow. He also adds the net margin he makes on an average order to the campaign as a monetary value. After a few weeks, Brad goes in to assess the results. There are three areas that are useful to him:

✧ Site referrer data. By selecting Traffic sources > Referring sites, Brad can see which of the two ezines has sent him more traffic.
✧ Campaign data. Under Traffic sources > Campaigns, Brad can see how many users were sent from the two sites when compared to his other campaigns. He can drill down on this campaign to find out more, including goal conversion. From the goals menu, he can analyze points in the customer journey where most users exited ("abandoned funnels") and look at the "reverse path" taken by those who did complete successfully.
✧ Site overlay data. From Content > Overview > Site overlay, Brad can view a visualization of how users navigate through his site. This is conceivably Google Analytics' single most useful feature for webmasters serious about driving up their conversions.

As a result of this analysis, Brad gets one of the ezine webmasters to repoint his link at a new landing page, where he undertakes A/B split testing on a new approach with a more prominent call to action, less text, and bigger Buy now buttons. This improves his conversions. Eventually Brad drops one of the ezines as the ROI is insufficient to cover his costs, but he does successfully advertise on two new sites with the benefit of a much better idea of what works.

7.2 Google Webmaster Tools

I covered the process of verifying your site for Google Webmaster Tools earlier (page 65). However, you can do a lot more with the console than simply sitemap submission. For example, you can see how Googlebot is crawling your site and investigate both your best rankings on Google and which of those delivers the most clicks. You can also look at the anchor text used in your inbound links. The service is enhanced on a regular basis and has become an invaluable toolset for webmasters.

Under "Diagnostics" you can:

- ✧ See when Google last crawled your site.
- ✧ See what crawl errors there have been.
- ✧ Check your robots.txt file.
- ✧ Request a different crawl rate.
- ✧ Sign up for the advanced image search function.
- ✧ Set a www preference for all your URLs (see below).

The last item requires a little further explanation. Some sites mix their use of the URL construction http://yourdomain.com and http://www.your domain.com. Other sites use these two constructions for different sites. Google has always struggled to tell the difference and passed PageRank separately to each. This led some search engine marketers to recommend using a 301 redirect (see page 81) to point all http:// pages to http://www, a very inefficient process. Google has added the preference setting to Webmaster Tools so that you no longer need a 301 redirect. You should set the preferred domain option to www unless you have a good reason to do otherwise.

Under "Statistics" you can see:

- ✧ The PageRank distribution of all your pages in Google.
- ✧ Top search queries for your site.
- ✧ Top search query clicks.
- ✧ Most used text in links to your site.
- ✧ Most used text on your pages.

Under "Links" you can see exactly how many inbound links there are to each of your pages in turn (from the full Google index, rather than just the sample you get from the link: operator). This is a very valuable tool.

7.3 Other useful tools

There are a number of other useful services across the web that you should look at.

Tracking Google PageRank (PR)

FORUM TOOLS — To find out the PageRank of any site, the best way is to download the Google Toolbar (http://toolbar.google.com) or use any of the popular online PageRank checkers. The forum (www.seo-expert-services.co.uk) provides a list.

The distribution of PageRank across the whole web follows a logarithmic pattern, where there are very few PR10 pages but hundreds of thousands of pages with a PR0. The PageRank system is actually a zero-sum game, in that any increase in the PR of one site is effectively offset by a tiny reduction in the PR of every other site, so that the average stays at 1). If you were to do nothing in terms of ongoing link building, you should expect your PageRank to decline gently over time. Indeed, as the web grows one would expect the number of pages with a very high PR to reduce and the benchmark for what constitutes a high PR in the first place to fall over time.

As we saw earlier in the book (page 128), to increase Google PageRank you need to get links from other sites into yours – and lots of them. Also, links from sites with higher PageRanks are worth more than ones with little or no PageRank. As an example, just one link from a PR10 webpage (if it's the only link on that page) would typically be enough to earn your linked page a PR8 in the next toolbar update, but you might need nearly 350,000 links from PR3 pages to achieve the same result.

Tracking keyword performance

Before the end of 2006, Google used to make available what were known as search API keys. By using an API key, programmers could directly access the Google index, bypassing in the process the Google search box. A number of developers created very cool tools to track search engine positions and perform many complex SEO tasks.

Unfortunately, Google decided to withdraw these keys and no longer provides support for them or offers the ability to obtain new ones (although you can get one for Google Maps). However, if you still have a search API key or can borrow or buy one, there are a number of useful tools that you can access to monitor where you rank in Google on certain keyphrases. These are listed opposite.

However, if you haven't got a Google API key, don't panic! Google continues to improve the rank-tracking functionality of Webmaster tools, which will in time make all other tools redundant.

Site/tool URL	Comments
www.googlerankings.com	See where you are in the top 1,000 for any given keyword phrase. Saves you tabbing through lots of SERPs pages yourself.
www.googlealert.com	Subscription required. Free trial allows you to track changes to the top 50 results for up to 5 keyphrases. Update report by email.
www.gorank.com	Perhaps the best of the lot, allowing you to track multiple keywords and competitors all on one page, and monitor trends in position.

Monitoring your traffic rank

In addition to commercial services such as Neilsen NetRatings, ComScore, and Hitwise, there are a number of free-to-use traffic rank-monitoring services. The best known of these are listed below:

Site URL	Comments	Est.	PR
www.alexa.com	Requires registration and claim code	1996	8
www.ranking.com	Requires registration. Small data set	1998	7
www.compete.com	Small data set	1995	6
www.quantcast.com	Very simple to use. Excellent quality	2005	7

To get started with Alexa, download and install the Alexa Toolbar from http://download.alexa.com. Tailored toward website owners and SEO freaks, Amazon-owned Alexa provides detailed statistics and information about the websites that a user visits. Alexa TrafficRank, like Google PageRank and Amazon SalesRank, follows a logarithmic scale where the top-placed site gets exponentially more traffic than, say, the site at position 500, which itself gets exponentially more traffic than the site at position 5,000.

Alexa computes traffic rankings by analyzing the aggregated historical traffic data from millions of Alexa Toolbar users. The main Alexa traffic rank reflects both the number of users who visit that site and the number of pages they then view. The former is termed reach and is expressed as the percentage of all internet users who visit the site. The latter, called page views, are a measure of unique daily visits, on average, by each user in the period under study. Alexa shows a daily, weekly, and three-monthly picture for any site and how these are trending over time. So, if a site like yahoo.com has a weekly reach of 28%, this means that in an average day during that week, 28% of all global internet users (measured by Alexa) visited it.

Alexa sounds good but it has a number of limitations, mainly due to the Toolbar population being unrepresentative of the internet user base as a whole. For example, the Alexa Toolbar is not supported on the AOL/Netscape and Opera browsers; Alexa users are disproportionately likely to visit sites that are featured on alexa.com, such as amazon.com and archive.org; and there is a strong relative uptake of Alexa in China and Korea. More importantly, the Alexa Toolbar is disproportionately used by webmasters with an unhealthy SEO obsession (like me!). Web directories, SEO blogs, and the like tend to have their traffic overstated.

The other key point is that the reliability of Alexa's data falls exponentially as you move down through the rankings. The data set is not large enough to determine accurately the rankings of sites with fewer than 1,000 total monthly visitors. Alexa itself states that the data for any site sitting outside the top 100,000 is inherently unreliable, due to a lack of statistical significance. Indeed, if your site is outside the top 1,000,000, you will notice that, as soon as you start looking at your site through Alexa, your site ranking seems to tick up. This is actually you affecting the numbers!

All the same, the Alexa data is the best of a bad lot, in my humble opinion. It may not be perfect, but it's a useful guide nonetheless to your position relative to your competitors. I would install the Alexa toolbar in your browser once every three to four months for a short period to check your position, then uninstall it until the next time you want to check, so that your own browsing doesn't skew the results too much.

Of the rest, by far the most promising is Quantcast.com. Try putting the following URL into the query box on the homepage:

http://quantcast.com/squidoo.com

As you can see, the site makes an impressive attempt at tracking the traffic to the site and giving usage demographics by gender, age, household income, and more. The tool also attempts to pattern match similar sites and rank keyword use. Quantcast still only contains a medium-sized data set but has the potential to trounce Alexa in the longer term.

Checking your backlinks

Many people use the link:www.yourdomain.com operator to check their inbound links from the Google index. However, this operator only works from a sample of your links and also filters out any internal links (within your site) or those that are similar. There is a more advanced hack known only to a few people (until now!) that will trick Google into giving you a more complete set of results. Enter into the query box your domain name with a plus sign inserted between the dot and the TLD domain extension:

yourdomain.+com

However, as I have said earlier in this section, the most reliable place to see all the links Google has recorded for you is to use the Google Webmaster Tools console.

Yahoo! also provides link data and Yahoo! SiteExplorer (which I first introduced you to in the sitemap submission section, page 65) is a useful place to cross-check your Webmaster Tools tally. Visit the Yahoo! homepage and type link:http://www.yourdomain.com into the search box. You will be redirected to results from the inbound link analyzer. Select the "Except from this domain" filter to show only links in from other sites than your own.

As you look through the results, you may notice that in some cases you get more than one link from different pages of the same domain. These extra links look nice on the total, but they do not really count with Google. What you want to see is unique inbound links, where each linking external domain is only counted once. You can establish this figure by exporting each of Yahoo's link results pages to a spreadsheet (using the "export to TSV" function) and deleting duplicate rows.

FORUM TOOLS So what about ongoing link monitoring and trend analysis? On the forum I provide up-to-date links to the best backlink-tracker tools around. However, I would like to draw your attention to the Market Leap Link Popularity Checker (see www. marketleap.com/publinkpop/default.htm).

Put in your homepage URL and those of up to three competitors, together with the best-fit market category for your business. Click Go to pick up composite backlink data from Google and Yahoo!. The results are divided into two tabs. The industry benchmark report places all four sites into six bands (from "limited presence" to "900lb gorilla"). The trend/history report shows how links are trending over time. Initially, trend data for you or your competitors may not be available. However, the very act of performing the query will nudge MarketLeap into gathering the data for all of the sites in future.

Tracking PageRank

As I have indicated previously, you can check your Google PageRank by using the Google Toolbar and there are various (generally unreliable) tools to predict where your PageRank might head in the future. You will have to work very hard indeed to get your PageRank up to a decent level.

Investing your time wisely is most important, or you could spend the rest of your natural life getting nowhere fast! Ideally, you want anchor-rich inbound links from sites with a homepage ranked PR5 or better, as then the odds become playable and worth the effort. Just be aware that as loads of other people know this too, your average PR6 website owner gets inundated with polite linking requests.

Also be aware that PageRank works in reverse for outbound links. If a PR6 site links to a PR0 site (such as your new one) it will dilute its own PageRank slightly, as well as present another opportunity for visitors to exit its site. Now who is going to do that just to help you out?

What you need to remember above all else is that PageRank is only relevant in ordering search results where sites have a similar search relevance for the words searched. In other words, PageRank is only likely to be very important to you if you are seeking to enter an extremely crowded marketplace (e.g., real estate) where there are already hundreds of established, optimized sites.

Interpreting your own web statistics

Don't neglect your own log files or site statistics in seeking to understand the success of your SEO strategy. If you don't already have a stats package installed, Google Analytics may be your best bet. Alternatively, check out one of the following:

- ✧ Webalizer - www.webalizer.com
- ✧ AWStats - http://awstats.sourceforge.net
- ✧ Analog/Report Magic - www.reportmagic.org

Ignore "hits" and "files." A <u>hit</u> is any element called by your browser when it requests a page. A <u>file</u> is a hit that actually returned data from the server. Given that a single page may register anything from a single hit to hundreds (if it contains lots of images or external scripts and style sheets), it is not very useful data for any kind of comparison.

Unique visitors are recorded through each new IP address that hits your site. This underestimates the total, as people visiting your site from the same IP address (such as those on an office network) will be counted as a single visitor. Repeat visitors are a subset of this, where the same IP address has been visited more than once (and will be overestimated for the same reasons highlighted above). If your visitor numbers are on the rise, the chances are that your SEO strategy is yielding results.

Page views or page impressions measure the number of pages people have visited. By dividing this by total visitor numbers, you can also derive the number of pages that the average visitor views. Page views can give you an idea of whether or not visitors are finding what they need on your site and progressing through it, or just viewing a single page and leaving.

The key measure for you is the referrer data, where the link that a visitor clicked on to arrive at your site is counted as a referrer or referring site. By tracking the number of referrals that you get each month from each search engine (and comparing this to their respective market shares), you can get an idea of how your performance is improving over time.

Search terms and search strings appear in the referring URL (the web address your visitor came from) and can tell you a lot about the keywords you have successfully optimized. You might find that you are getting traffic on some unexpected terms and failing on some that you hoped would do well. However, this could in fact mean that you have hit on some useful words that your competitors have missed. Feed your findings back into future SEO activities.

The browsers section typically shows you which search engine robots are visiting your site, how often, and with what result (i.e., how many pages they are viewing). If you spot any areas of underperformance, re-read the crawler guidance at the robot homepage to make sure there is nothing you are doing to impede the spidering of your site.

7.4 Tuning the campaign

As I have explained previously, building hundreds of links over a very short time, particularly with very little variation in the anchor or clickable text, is a risky and complacent strategy. Google is capable of algorithmically identifying such unnatural linking patterns.

It is much better to revisit your link building every three or four months over a period of up to two years, based on the rankings you are tracking. If you have a new site, use the allinanchor:yourkeyphrase operator to see where you may end up when you're free of Google's age-deflation factor. Where you are not yet achieving your targets, build further links until you are. Do so gently and systematically.

Learn from your own web statistics and from Google Analytics. Where you are already getting good traffic from a keyphrase, build around that. Equally, revisit your keyword analysis: Where you are missing out on a good stream of traffic that you know is there, keep up the fight until you gain some purchase.

Remember that websites and directories do close down or go out of business, and the links you used to have from them go too. Even sites that stay around refresh their pages from time to time. Your links may not survive the latest makeover. One thing is therefore certain: Were you to do nothing for a period of many months, the number of links to your site would gradually decline, and your rankings with them. It is vital to maintain your position through periodic tuning and maintenance.

Getting to the top

Getting to the top on Google is literally a make-or-break mission for your business. More than 80% of first visits for a typical site are derived from search engines and of those, more than 75% come from Google's properties worldwide. As we have seen, 84% of searchers on Google never make it past the second page of the results and 65% hardly ever click on paid or sponsored results.

As you will have noted throughout the guide, search engine optimization is a multifaceted activity. It is likely to be time-consuming, and it is important that you spend that time wisely. Nothing you do will be without merit, so spread your effort across a broad range of valid, ethical SEO tactics. Don't become obsessed with any one method and always do everything in moderation. Above all, remember that SEO is only one aspect of marketing, which itself is only one aspect of running a good business. Search engine optimization is a means to an end, not an end in itself!

Seven top tips for success

As a summary, here are my seven top tips for search engine success:

1 <u>Find a great niche and create great content</u>. Give your users good reasons to come back and to bookmark, tag, and link to your site. If you do only this and nothing else, your site will rank well without any specific optimization activity. (See Step 1.)

2 <u>Lay the right foundations</u>. Host your site with a fast and flexible provider, and structure the site symmetrically and with a logical domain name, directory structure, and filenames. (See Step 2.)

3 <u>Do everything you can with the assets under your control</u> in terms of on-page SEO, but realize that this only gets you to the

start line in the race for decent rankings. SEO is not simply an exercise in decent copywriting. (See Step 3.)

4 <u>Spend more time on directory submissions, article writing, and online press releases.</u> Provide a hook. Your site must be news-worthy, funny, or controversial, or at the very least full of great resources. (See Step 4.)

5 <u>By all means use paid advertising, but only as an adjunct to a decent organic search campaign</u> (rather than the other way around). Save money by targeting long-tail terms, tuning match drivers, and crafting decent landing pages. (See Step 5.)

6 If your business has a local angle, <u>put some focus into local directory listings, geo-targeting, language optimization, and Google Earth/KML optimization.</u> As the web gets more local, your investment will pay dividends. (See Step 6.)

7 If you can, <u>create a business advisory blog</u> and make it easy for others to tag and syndicate your content and products. Increase your presence on wikis, lenses, and other social networking sites to futureproof your rankings. (See Step 4.)

Search engine optimization is not rocket science! Many of the tech-niques I have outlined are straightforward enough. The key is to outstay your competitors and have patience. Keep doing the right things often enough and the ranking benefits will come.

Continuing your journey – the SEO Expert Forum

Remember, the world of SEO changes fast and with new developments come fresh opportunities to pull ahead from your competitors. Don't forget to sign up for the SEO Expert Forum at www.seo-expert-services.co.uk and claim your six months of free membership. On the forum you will be able to collaborate with other webmasters and pose questions directly to me through the "Ask the expert" function.

I hope that you have found *Get to the Top on Google* useful and that as a result you enjoy some positive effects over time in your search engine results and web traffic. This book should pay for itself many times over through your increased revenue and profitability online. Do visit the forum at www.seo-expert-services.co.uk and let me know how you get on – and keep an eye out for future updated editions of this guide.

Index